marathon manual

marathon manual

cathy shipton with liz mccolgan

cartoons by candy guard

with co-operation from the

British Heart Foundation
The heart research charity

Thorsons
An Imprint of HarperCollins*Publishers*

for dad

Thorsons
An Imprint of HarperCollins*Publishers*
77–85 Fulham Palace Road
Hammersmith, London W6 8JB
1160 Battery Street
San Francisco, California 94111–1213

Published by Thorsons 1997

10 9 8 7 6 5 4 3 2 1

A catalogue record for this book
is available from the British Library

ISBN 0 7225 3342 X

Cartoons by Candy Guard
Text illustrations by Jennie Dooge and Peter Cox

Printed and bound in Great Britain by
Scotprint Ltd, Musselburgh, Edinburgh

contents

acknowledgements

for their much appreciated help, I wish to thank Liz and Peter McColgan, Eamonn Martin, Geoff Wightman, Tom Knight, Gordon Surtees, John Hanscomb and all at Ranelagh Harriers, Leslie Watson, John Milbourne, Neil Fennell, Dr Tunstall Pedoe, FRCP, DPhil, Dr Gilbert Thompson, Dr Adriann Hardman, Alan Watson, Hilary Kingsley, David Bryant, Alan Rustad, my agent Jane Bradish-Ellames and my publisher Wanda Whiteley. A special thanks to Chris for being my inspiration and support in running and with this book.

The support of the British Heart Foundation in supplying information and advice about heart disease and a healthier lifestyle is gratefully acknowledged.

introduction

training for a marathon can be a lonely affair. However many of us there are out there and however much good advice we may get, we runners are ultimately on our own. For me this is at once the beauty and the dilemma of distance running.

Sound, objective, scientifically based guidelines are of course essential to anyone who is serious about any athletic endeavour. But without a personal philosophy and a sense of humour, the technical information alone can leave you feeling very isolated.

My early training experiences were sometimes frustrating because I tended to apply objective standards to my progress without listening to myself at the same time. It was not until I began to talk openly not only to other fun runners but also to élite athletes that I realized I was not alone in my dilemma. They, like me, have had to come to terms with their own individual quirks and inconsistencies and by learning to understand themselves better, have set themselves free to realize their own individual potential. For me the key to successful distance training is a flexible balance between technical objectivity and personal self-awareness. Most of us do not have the luxury of one-to-one coaching, so the aim of this book is not only to provide information but also to encourage each of us to become our own very personal trainer.

one **the decision**

it seems that most of us are running most of the time. We're running a business, running a temperature, running for a bus or running behind schedule. If you are literally running, you might also be doing one if not all of the above. In the last 20 years or so a lot of people have taken up running as their preferred way to keep fit, and regular vigorous exercise certainly does that. But what makes seemingly balanced individuals want to run 26.2 miles?

The answer is obvious if you are an élite athlete training hard and competing against the world's best to break records and make your mark in sporting history. But they only make up a tiny percentage of the numbers that turn out to take part in marathons all over the world. The vast majority, the massed runners, come in all shapes and sizes, from all walks of life, all with the same purpose: to get round the course in their own personal best time.

One day, many months – and in some cases many years – before you set out on the race you will have made a decision to do it. For me there was a 14-year gap between the dream and the reality. But it had always been there somewhere inside me. Of course the desire to raise money for the British Heart Foundation was a strong incentive, but looking back it was as if time had stood still and the doing was all.

Making the Commitment

Whatever your reason, once you have decided to run a marathon, things will never be quite the same again. Acting on your decision can be hard because it incurs inevitable changes which can only be accommodated with time and patience. You may not be so available to family, friends and work associates, and even when you are you may be tired and sore and not in the mood for socializing. Runners can become quite zealous creatures, sometimes getting such a buzz from running that other activities seem unimportant. There are times when a runner is moody and irritable because he or she is pushing hard but falling short of targets. That's when a sense of humour is useful and some time spent in contemplation is essential. Never underestimate the commitment required to get through the intensive training a marathon demands.

This isn't meant to put you off, but you do have to ask yourself some hard questions. Take a good look at your lifestyle and how your time is divided up, then carefully work out the best times to train. It's no good running when you think you should be doing something else. The last thing you need to spoil your fun is a head full of guilty worries! In fact one of the things I love most about running is the freedom it gives me. There are no distractions, no telephones, no demands apart from those I choose to make of myself. Running is simply running. You can do it anywhere, anytime – and no matter how bad you feel when you set out, the effort is usually worth it. By the time you get back you feel ready to face anything – well, almost anything – the world can throw at you.

Tell your family and friends what you intend to do – you'll not only need them in the crowd on race day, but they'll also be an invaluable source of support all through your training. Most people are impressed to know someone who is going to run a marathon and their enthusiasm will help to nurture your self-esteem. Knowing what you are letting yourself in for helps, too, so gather as much information as you can to work out realistic times and targets. The key to self-motivation during a training programme is to set yourself attainable goals and then, encouraged by each achievement, you will feel the desire to carry on.

Making Plans...

If you are a beginner, it is wise to proceed with caution and allow yourself a lot of leeway. Read the section devoted to new runners, which has a programme designed to introduce you to running, before going into full marathon training (see pp.10–25). If you are looking to improve your times, you may wish to include more training sessions and different training techniques. But remember this will require more time and more rest, so always try to think a new schedule through before embarking on it.

Another effective way of maintaining morale is to join a running club. Here you can benefit from the wisdom of seasoned athletes as well as sharing your experiences with people at your own level. You will pick up a lot of training tips and discover the social side of running, too. Throughout the training period it will be necessary to enter a few races, especially if you are a beginner, and one way of getting race information is through a club.

However, whether you train with a club or simply with a friend, you are always on your own. When it comes to race day, you may not be running with the people you know and isolation can lead to anxiety, so as you are training, always listen first and last to yourself. Then on race day, run for yourself and you will enjoy the marathon experience to the full.

SUMMING UP

- Write down why you want to run a marathon, however obvious the reasons, e.g. for charity, as well as the more personal reasons.
- Gather as much information about training as you can and work out how long a period of training you will require.
- Look at your lifestyle and be realistic about whether you can fit the training in.
- Tell your family and friends what you intend to do, and ask for their help.
- Join a club or find a running partner.
- Promise yourself to take it seriously ... but not too seriously!

two running – the benefits

regular, dynamic exercise such as running has well documented beneficial effects on our bodies as well as our minds. It is also a fact that physical inactivity is common in Britain and that although people are aware of the health benefits of exercise, they choose to do little or nothing about it.

Dr Dan Tunstall Pedoe, FRCP, DPhil, Senior Lecturer and Consultant in Medicine and Cardiology at St Bartholomew's Hospital, London, has been the Medical Director to the London Marathon since it started in 1981 and is a keen runner himself. He has advised runners at all levels for many years and believes that if you train properly you will derive great benefit from your running programme. Here are his views on the benefits of running:

■ Running tends to make people more aware of their lifestyle. You can gradually put on weight over a period of time as you become less active. These changes sometimes happen without you even noticing. People who run and exercise regularly are naturally more aware of their health, their weight and lifestyle, and less likely to suffer coronary heart disease – CHD.

Runners are far less likely to smoke. Women find it harder to stop smoking than men, yet their chances of quitting are enhanced once they start an exercise routine. During training your heart rate naturally increases, causing the muscles of the heart to become stronger and more efficient. As a consequence your heart rate is slower at rest and during normal activities – your heart is becoming healthier and has to do less work to achieve the same results.

Running regularly can slightly reduce your blood pressure, perhaps by a few points, and if you suffer with marginal hypertension this can be sufficient to take you off medication.

As a runner, you will start to increase your ratio of good cholesterol – high density lipoprotein (HDL) – to bad cholesterol – low density lipoprotein (LDL) [see Cholesterol, p.77.

Although the tests aren't as yet conclusive, running will probably reduce your chances of developing diabetes. The intense physical activity will burn up any excess fat and so prevent the condition of adult onset diabetes.

Studies have shown that your chances of stroke in later life are greatly reduced if you are active when young, and following an exercise programme can seriously reduce your risk of CHD and sudden death.

Additional benefits for runners are the maintenance of a desirable body weight, a delay in the onset of fatigue and improved endurance. This means that you can cope better with the demands of everyday life, being lighter, fitter and more energetic.

There are very clear psychological benefits from following a training programme. If you are mildly depressed, running elevates your mood. If you are not depressed, running improves your body image. The feeling of achievement can boost your self-esteem and confidence, which has a positive effect on your life and relationships.

Women benefit from high-impact exercise like running, as it increases the bone density. In the last 40–50 years there has been an increase in osteoporosis – thin bones that fracture and break easily in mature women. It is believed that this condition has come about because women work less physically hard due to all the labour saving devices. Bone density is improved through any exercise that places a stress on the bones in the legs and spine such as high-impact aerobics, step aerobics and running.

Regular running can also have a positive effect on your sex life. This is because you have an improved body image and experience feelings of well-being and achievement. Your body is physically stronger and your mind is less stressed, leaving you free to enjoy other physical activities!

The media make a lot of marathon runners collapsing and the public is given the impression that marathon running is inherently dangerous. The reality is very different. The common medical risks of marathon running and training are not alarming and can be prevented. Women may suffer amenorrhoea (temporary loss of periods), but to date the commonest reason for withdrawal from the London Marathon is pregnancy. Most runners suffer blisters and friction chafing, which can be alleviated by vaseline; some may have developed a chronic joint problem which causes them to be a casualty on the day. Major trauma such as heart attack is extremely uncommon and there have been four deaths in 15 years out of 300,000 runners of average age 39–40.

Organizers of marathon events cannot be responsible for your health and the idea of screening every entrant is unfeasible and possibly inaccurate. Many people choose to ignore the signals their bodies send them, as they get so obsessed with running. Never train or race if you are unwell. Heed your body; there will always be another race. ■

What Happens When You Run

In order to perform any activity there is a sequence of functions that the body must perform. You breathe in oxygen from the air, which is then absorbed into the blood and transported to the muscles that require it. The heart, blood vessels, lungs and circulatory system work together at different levels, depending on the amount of work we want them to do and how fit we are.

THE EFFECTS OF TRAINING

The aim of a training programme for an endurance runner is to gradually increase the load placed on the heart and lungs, bringing about greater efficiency.

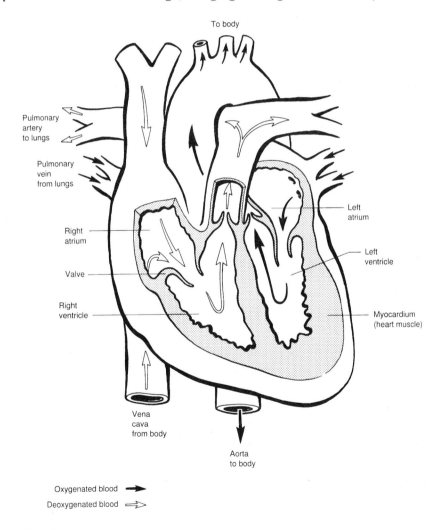

The cardiopulmonary system.

A trained runner can inhale 6 litres of air with a single breath; an untrained person can only manage about 5 litres. When a trained runner is pushing hard in a session or a race, the oxygen uptake dramatically increases to almost twice that of an untrained person. This is called the maximal aerobic capacity, or VO_2 max – the amount of oxygen taken from the blood for use in the muscles in a given period of time. In order to ascertain your actual aerobic capacity you would need to be measured running on a treadmill while breathing into devices that measure gas volume.

TRAINING AND THE HEART

Training also brings about a thickening and strengthening of the muscle fibres that surround the heart. This enables the heart to pump more blood with each stroke. Blood contains haemoglobin, which is essential for carrying oxygen, and trained runners also have more red blood cells. So training leads to a greater uptake of oxygen which is then absorbed and transported more quickly and efficiently to the muscles than would occur in an untrained person. There is a proliferation of the blood vessels in the muscles, which increases the supply of oxygen and nutrients to the muscle cells. During rest the muscles require about 1 l/minute of blood flow. However, when you run, that blood flow can increase to 12 l/minute.

Regular running decreases the risk of CHD, sudden death and angina. This is because the increased blood flow through the heart protects it by increasing the efficiency of the blood circulation and allowing the heart rate to be slower at rest. The heart benefits from these improvements both at rest and during exertion. Running will also prevent a furring up of the arteries and keep down body fat, thus guarding a normal person against high cholesterol, hypertension and diabetes.

THE OXYGEN DEBT

When you first start running or start to increase your distances you may experience the need, during a session, to go slower, as if your muscles can't go on. What has happened is the muscles cannot get enough oxygen to run at the pace you want them to, so instead of functioning aerobically (with oxygen), they are functioning anaerobically (without oxygen). It is at this stage that you are said to have an 'oxygen debt' and a substance called lactic acid accumulates in the muscles. Slowing your pace allows oxygen to be transported to the muscles at a more compatible rate, so the supply doesn't outweigh the demand.

The process of improving your performance as a runner therefore depends on increasing your aerobic capacity and building up skeletal muscle strength. Training imposes a controlled amount of stress on your body, which gradually adapts to it, and so you increase your level of fitness. This way you can go from being out of breath running for a bus to comfortably running a marathon in six months.

FUEL

The whole system also has to be fuelled with the proper nutrition in order to be able to undertake this workload. This fuel will supply the body with energy.

Energy isn't stored up in the body, but is released through a chemical process as and when required. All muscle cells contain a substance that can convert the energy derived from our digested food and release it for the body's processes and activities.

ATP, adenosine triphosphate, is the only substance in the body able to do this. Its molecular structure is adenosine with three phosphate groups attached:

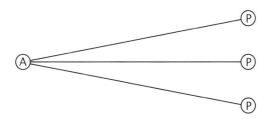

The chemical bonds between these phosphate groups are called 'high energy bonds' and when they are broken, energy is released. The resulting molecule is ADP, or adenosine diphosphate. Once the released energy has been used, the ADP is converted back to ATP and so the cycle continues.

The body has enough ATP to produce energy to support life. Anything requiring more energy will naturally require more fuel. We will look at the best fuel to run on in Chapter 8.

Training for a marathon will help you examine your current lifestyle and the programme will offer suggestions that will not only get you through a marathon, but also live a longer, healthier life.

three **new runners**

so, you have responded to a dare, or wish to fulfil a personal challenge,
and you want to run a marathon. To be absolutely realistic, the longer you
can give yourself to train and prepare, the better. However, being equally
realistic, life doesn't always go like that. The best time to start training
is when you apply for a place, and for a high profile race that could
be at least 10 months before you will run. A lot of
people enter and don't do anything about it
until they are accepted; depending on
your age, state of health and level of
fitness, this might also be alright.

**Amazed, shattered, relieved! You're in!
Now there's the small matter of
running 26.2 miles**

Ideally, after applying for a place, if you are new to any form of exercise, are over 40, have a sedentary lifestyle or have had any major illness or surgery in the last five years, get checked out by your GP. Once you get the go ahead, start training as soon as you can.

FITNESS TEST

You may be interested at this stage to put yourself through a fitness test *(see pp. 16–25)*. This will give you a general but realistic idea of your level of fitness – and you might be surprised at the results.

The next thing is to get yourself equipped. The following chapter will advise you as to everything you'll need *(see pp.26–42)*.

The Schedule

Eight-Week Beginners Get Fit to Run Schedule
(all values are in running minutes)

	Sun	Mon	Tue	Wed	Thur	Fri	Sat
Week 1	5	5	10	5	8	5	8
Week 2	12	5	10	8	10	5	8
Week 3	15	8	12	5	10	8	10
Week 4	15	8	15	5	10	8	12
Week 5	17	10	15	8	12	5	15
Week 6	20	10	15	10	17	rest	15
Week 7	20	10	15	12	15	rest	17
Week 8	25	15	20	12	15	rest	20

The schedule is designed on a weekly basis which can be adjusted to suit your particular week, but don't swap the running minutes around within the week. This schedule will bring you up to a level of fitness to start the marathon training programme. If you have longer than eight weeks, you can repeat the last two weeks as often as you like – every day will see an improvement as you get stronger and fitter.

This is the period of time that you will spend running on your own or perhaps with a friend or partner, building up the time you can comfortably spend on your feet, prior to joining a club. Do not worry about working out distances, as you will be running to time. You will soon be able to assess your progress as you watch yourself covering old routes a lot quicker.

When you look at the time spent running in the first few weeks you may feel the urge to skip on through the week to a higher time – resist this temptation! There is a progressive workload built in to the schedule, and the aim isn't to set off and see how long you can run for, it's to gradually accustom the body to the action of running. These early days are so valuable. You can take your time to develop your running style.

Arrange your day to include running, then set the time aside and keep to it. The best way is to run at the same time each day. If that means in your lunch-time, make sure you can have a shower afterwards. You won't get much encouragement from your work-mates otherwise!

Having got a good pair of running shoes and the appropriate clothing, you can't put it off any longer – it's time to start.

WARMING UP

You may feel that it is slightly ridiculous spending 5–10 minutes warming up to then go out and run for only 5–10 minutes. But what you are doing is setting up good habits that are respectful to your body. This short time spent stretching your muscles and moving your joints will become a vital part of running, both mentally and physically, as the time and distance increases. You are simply saying to yourself, 'I have stopped one activity [driving, working or cooking, etc.] and I am now getting ready to do another.'

If exercise is a thing of the past, or you are a beginner, it's advisable to study the warm up and cool down exercises in advance so that you can learn what exercise is affecting which muscle group. Once you have absorbed the information your warm up/cool down routine will be second nature. See Chapter 5 for the full routine (pp.43–59).

PACE

Your aim when you run is to feel as natural and easy as possible. The 'talk test' is a good way to check how you are feeling: you should be able to run at a pace comfortable enough to be able to talk. If you are out of breath, slow down. Suppress the urge to set off like a greyhound from the slips as you might only get to the end of the street with chronic stitch, a red face – and another four minutes to go!

Believe me – I've done it. I used to feel very self-conscious when I ran and would make a supreme effort to look like a runner. Big mistake. Runners just run, they don't really care what they look like. After this supreme effort of one whole minute I would still have to go around the block to get home and I would spend the remaining four minutes puffing and panting, looking at my watch every 30 seconds, praying for it to be over and finally collapsing in a purple heap outside the front door. I used to set off so badly and with no plan, it's little wonder I gave up running so many times!

GIVE YOURSELF A BREAK

Don't be hard on yourself. You will soon be training for an endurance event, not the 100 metres, and you have to start somewhere.

If at any time during a run you feel too tired to go on, don't stop – just slow down to a jog or a walk and run again when you are ready. Similarly there will be times when you feel a rush of energy – so go with it, it's for free and a terrific feeling when your pace naturally picks up.

Initially you may also experience twinges of pain in the Achilles tendons, calves or hamstrings. This is quite normal, as the body is learning to deal with the new activity and you do have to push through a certain amount of stiffness and soreness. It may also be a sign that you are not warming up properly. Cramps and stitches are also common and will wear off during the run.

If, however, at any time you experience pain in the muscles or joints such as pulls and tears or sprains and strains, then stop immediately and assess the problem *(see Injuries, pp.89–104).*

RUNNING STYLE

Running is the most natural activity in the world – most of us do it before we walk. If you watch a child at play he or she will run up to you, get a cuddle, run off again, stop suddenly to investigate something, jump up, skip over to a pal, grab a toy and run off. Children never stop, and their instincts and curiosity guide them. Why not do the same? When you set out running for the first time, just let it happen naturally with as little tension throughout the body as possible and with minimum effort.

You don't want to spend too much time watching yourself, but here are a few pointers to help you run smoothly and efficiently:

- **Always run heel through toe. Running on your toes is very tiring and can place undue strain on your muscles and tendons. Most people strike the ground first with the heel and the outside of the foot, then rotate on to the ball of the foot to move forward. There is a kind of rocking movement till the lift off at the toe.**

- **Alignment through the body is important – you want to run with the feet parallel, as if there were a line linking hip, knee and foot. Any slight deviation from this, such as knock knees or splayed feet, can affect the ease with which you run and result in injury. This alignment carries through to the upper body: you want to keep your back straight and your head held easily without jutting from the chin or forehead. Try not to lean forward from the waist, as this makes you overbalance and could give you** backache. New runners can have a tendency to 'sit down' as they run, putting their weight behind them. So while keeping the body erect, don't drop your weight by keeping your hips forward.

A good running position.

■ Let your arms find a position that is comfortable; you don't have to pump them hard unless you are pushing up a hill, which you won't be doing at this stage. Your arms offer balance to the body, working in the opposite way to your legs. They should swing forwards rather than sideways, with the elbows in and the hands relaxed and cupped. Let the arms find their natural rhythm as you run.

■ A lot of new runners find that they accumulate tension in the head, neck and shoulder area. Try to relax as far as possible when you run, and if you feel tension creeping in, shake out your shoulders and neck. If your jaw feels clenched, relax it and gently move it from side to side.

■ It isn't necessary to think about your stride length at this stage – the pace you choose will decide the length of stride that is best for you.

LIZ: 'Running with a friend or training partner can be great. You can compare notes, offer encouragement, pool ideas and obviously keep each other company. Safety should always be uppermost in your mind, for everybody but especially for women. If at all possible, never run on your own and run on familiar routes along well-lit streets. If you do run off-road, keep together, and tell those at home where you are running and roughly when to expect you back. All this may sound a bit gloomy, but it's really just a matter of common sense.'

Keep your routes to flat, level surfaces at this stage and if possible vary road with grass to limit the stress factor on the body. Grass is by far the most preferable surface, however you will eventually be running a road race, so you do have to put in road miles.

RUNNING DIARY

This is a good time to start your running diary – a simple exercise book will do to record your times and thoughts. It can prove such a source of satisfaction as the weeks go by, giving you a tangible record of all the ups and downs. Eamonn Martin's running diary will give you some inspiration *(see pp.131–132)*. Your own diary will put all your efforts in perspective. *For more information, see the following chapter, p.26.*

COOLING DOWN

Finally, follow the cool down exercises to ease the body out of running mode and stretch the worked muscles *(see pp.51–58)*. You will probably notice that after you have run, your body is warmed up and it is easier to hold the exercise positions. I have also suggested several yoga positions that in time you may wish to introduce into your cool down.

There's no getting away from it – you will be sore and stiff! But stretching will stop the muscles seizing up and a long soak in a hot bath is guaranteed to work wonders.

How Fit Are You Really? /1

Many people have an unrealistic idea of their level of fitness. Some take a lot of exercise without thinking about it, more take a little exercise and believe themselves ultra-fit. Fitness is a combination of heart and muscle capacity to use oxygen for energy production. To find out how you rate, try these tests. Your scores will immediately reveal those areas in which you need to improve your performance.

Q

TEST 1

What is your resting pulse rate?
Your resting pulse is a simple and accurate gauge of cardiovascular fitness. As your fitness level increases, your resting pulse rate will become slower, stronger and more regular. Take your pulse when you wake up in the morning because any form of emotional or physical exertion will affect it during the day. Individual rates vary, but as a general rule, women have a slightly higher pulse rate than men. If you find your resting pulse is over 100 beats a minute, consult your doctor immediately.

Take your pulse at your wrist (at the base of your thumb) or by feeling the artery in your neck, which is located below the ear and toward the jawbone.

Resting pulse rate

Age	20–29	30–39	40–49	50+
Men				
Excellent	59 or less	63 or less	65 or less	67 or less
Good	60–69	64–71	66–73	68–75
Fair	70–85	72–85	74–89	76–89
Poor	86+	86+	90+	90+
Women				
Excellent	71 or less	71 or less	73 or less	75 or less
Good	72–77	72–79	74–79	76–83
Fair	78–95	80–97	80–98	84–102
Poor	96+	98+	99+	103+

TEST 2

What is your heart recovery time?

Try this simple step test to assess your aerobic fitness and stamina. The test reveals how efficiently your heart and lungs feed oxygen to your body by measuring the time it takes to slow down after it has speeded up for exercise. If your resting pulse rate is over 100 beats a minute, do not attempt this test.

Step onto a stair about 20 cm (8 in) high, then step down again, moving one foot after the other. Repeat 24 times a minute for 3 minutes. Stop and take your pulse. After resting for 30 seconds, take your pulse again and consult the chart.

Repeat this test after a few weeks of training and see if your heart recovers more quickly. The heart's natural capacity declines with age, so beware of exceeding the safe limit as you grow older. If at any moment you feel dizzy, nauseated or painfully breathless, stop *immediately*.

A

Recovery pulse rate at 30 seconds

Age	20–29	30–39	40–49	50+
Men				
Excellent	74 or less	78 or less	80 or less	83 or less
Good	75–84	79–86	81–88	84–90
Fair	85–100	87–100	89–104	91–104
Poor	101+	101+	105+	105+
Women				
Excellent	86 or less	86 or less	88 or less	90 or less
Good	87–92	87–94	89–94	91–98
Fair	93–110	95–112	95–114	99–116
Poor	111+	113+	115+	117+

Q

TEST 3

What is your safe maximum pulse rate?

Age	20–29	30–39	40–49	50+
Men	170	160	150	140
Women	170	160	150	140

Q

TEST 4

How active are you?
How often do you take physical exercise (including keep fit classes and sport) that makes you out of breath?

a   Four times or more a week
b   Two to three times a week
c   Once a week
d   Less than once a week

How far do you walk each day?

a   More than 5 km (3 miles)
b   Up to 5 km (3 miles)
c   Less than 1.6 km (1 mile)
d   Less than 0.8 km (½ mile)

How do you travel to work/the shops?

a   All the way by foot/cycle
b   Part of the way by foot/cycle
c   Occasionally by foot/cycle
d   All the way by public transport or car

When there is a choice do you:

a   Take the stairs – up and down – always
b   Take the stairs unless you have something to carry
c   Occasionally take the stairs
d   Take the lift/escalator unless it is broken

At weekends do you:

a   Spend several hours gardening/decorating/doing DIY/doing some sport
b   Usually only sit down for meals and in the evening
c   Take a few short walks
d   Spend most of the time sitting reading/watching TV

Do you think nothing of:

a   Doing the household chores after a day's work
b   Rushing out to the shops again if you have forgotten something
c   Getting other people to run your errands, even if you have the time
d   Paying for a telephone call when you could make a personal visit

A

Add up your score, allowing

4 points for every a answer
3 points for every b answer
2 points for every c answer
1 point for every d answer

20+

You are naturally very active and probably quite fit.

15–20

You are active and have a healthy attitude toward fitness.

10–15

You are only mildly active and would benefit from some more exercise.

Under 10

You are rather lazy and need to rethink your attitude toward activity. Try to reorganize your day to allow for some exercise.

Q

TEST 5

What can you do?

How long does it take you to:

1   *Walk 5 km (3 miles) on level ground:*
   a   1 hour 15 min (or more)
   b   50 min to 1 hour 10 min
   c   45 min (or less)
2   *Swim 1,000 m (1,000 yards):*
   a   50 min (or more)
   b   40 min
   c   20 min (or less)
3   *Run 1.6 km (1 mile) on level ground:*
   a   15 min (or more)
   b   9–14 min
   c   8 min (or less)

A

Scores

a   If you have covered the distance you have made a start. Now keep it up until the test feels easy.

b   You are moderately fit. If you want to improve, increase the distance and speed up gradually.

c   You have reached a good level of fitness and are ready to start a more vigorous fitness programme.

How Fit Are You Really? /2

Strength and flexibility are two important adjuncts to all-round fitness. Similarly, being the correct weight for your size is also conducive to good health. Obesity and lack of flexibility can impair mobility; additionally, obesity is associated with diabetes, with diseases of the gall bladder, heart and arteries, and with some kinds of cancer.

The tests given here offer some quick ways of finding out what shape you are in. Retake all the tests regularly and chart your progress over a period of many weeks. You should be encouraged by your advancement as you look back at your early efforts.

Q

TEST 1

Are you carrying unwanted fat?
Pinch yourself at the waist and on your upper arm, grasping as much flesh as possible between your finger and thumb.

A

If you can pinch more than about 2.5 cm (1 inch) of spare flesh, then this is an indication that you need to lose some fat. This may be a matter of merely toning up – replacing fat with muscle – or of losing weight. As a rule of thumb, every 0.6 cm (¼ inch) over 2.5 cm (1 inch) on this test represents about 4.5 kg (10 lb) of body fat.

Q

TEST 2

How am I changing?
Men and women tend to accumulate excess fat in different parts of their bodies. In men, flab is more likely round the waist, shoulders and upper arms. In women, waist, hips, thighs and bust are most prone to the build up of unwanted fat.

Measure yourself with a tape measure. If you are a man, measure your waist, upper arm, forearm and hips. If you are a woman, measure your waist, upper arm, forearm, thighs, calves and bust. Make a note of your findings along with the date. Measure in the same places each week and chart your progress.

If you are a man, breathe out, then, keeping your muscles relaxed, measure (or get someone else to measure) your waist at the level of your navel. Then breathe in and measure the circumference of your chest when your lungs are at their fullest.

If the waist measurement is more than the chest one, then you are carrying too much fat around your waist. Repeat the measurements weekly.

If you are a regular swimmer, find a place in the pool where you have a clear view of the second hand on a clock, or enlist the help of a friend with a watch that measures in seconds. Float on your back, but do not paddle with your hands to keep you buoyant. Empty your lungs by breathing out as far as you can. Time how long it takes you to sink. As you lose unwanted fat you will find that your buoyancy decreases. (This will not, incidentally, reduce your swimming efficiency.)

Q

TEST 3

How efficient are your lungs?
These quick tests give a rough guide to the efficiency with which your lungs are functioning. You need to have a laboratory test to measure this accurately.

Take a deep breath in and time how long you can hold your breath.

Breathe in and out as far as you can and measure your chest in each position.

A

If you can hold your breath for 45 seconds or more, and if the difference between the two chest measurements is 5–7½ cm (2–3 inches) or more, then it is likely that your lungs are working with adequate efficiency.

TEST 4

How flexible are you?

Flexibility is an important attribute for *all* physical activities. In particular, tight leg and back muscles impede movement in many sports and can cause back pain and stiffness after exercise. Women tend to be more supple than men and peak at the age of 15 to 19, several years before men, and decline more gradually.

To test your flexibility, attach some string or a stick firmly to the ground and sit down with your heels touching this line and your feet comfortably apart. Keeping your legs straight, bend forward slowly from the waist and reach as far as you can without straining. Place a marker at this point and relax. Take a ruler or measuring stick and measure the distance between your marker and the line. Score a plus (+) figure if it lies *beyond* your heel line and a minus (–) figure if it does not.

A

Men

Stretch rating	Age up to 35		Age 36–45		Age 45+	
	cm	in	cm	in	cm	in
Excellent	+6	1½	+5	2	+4	1½
Good	–3	1¼	+2	¾	+1	½
Fair	–5	2	–5	2	–6	2½
Poor	–8	3¼	–10	4	–10	4

Women

Stretch rating	Age up to 35		Age 36–45		Age 45+	
	cm	in	cm	in	cm	in
Excellent	+8	3¼	+7	2¾	+6	2½
Good	+5	2	+4	1½	+3	1¼
Fair	–1	½	–3	1¾	–2	¾
Poor	–4	1½	–5	2	–6	2½

How strong are you?

Muscular endurance is necessary for fitness because muscular effort has to be sustained without fatigue if aerobic fitness is to be maintained. Thus it is important for general fitness and a prerequisite for good performance in many sports and activities. One method of measuring strength is by your ability to do sit-ups.

How to do sit-ups

Lie on your back with your knees bent and your feet flat, or held flat by another person. Put your arms behind your head and, tightening your stomach, pull yourself up to a sitting position, using the strength of your stomach muscles. See how many sit-ups you can manage within 60 seconds and consult the chart to measure your result. Men generally have greater muscular endurance than women, but reach a peak a few years later, usually between the ages of 15 and 19.

A

Assess your performance

Men

Age	Muscular endurance		
	Excellent	**Good**	**Poor**
12–14	45	35	25
15–19	50	40	30
20–29	40	30	20
30–39	35	25	20
40–49	30	20	15
50–59	25	15	10
60–69	23	13	8

Women

Age	Muscular endurance		
	Excellent	**Good**	**Poor**
12–14	44	34	24
15–19	40	30	20
20–29	33	23	13
30–39	27	17	12
40–49	22	12	7
50–59	20	10	5
60–69	17	7	4

Source: *The BUPA Manual of Fitness and Wellbeing*; H. Beric Wright, MB, FRCS, MFOM, Consultant Editor

four the preparation

as with many things in life, you can get more out of running if you are prepared. In fact the easiest way to put yourself off running for good is to set out willy-nilly, with no thought as to when, where and for how long you are going to run. Doing precisely that is also how a lot of people incur injury. I want to look at several areas that are worth considering when you start running.

Health

Without a doubt committing yourself to a training programme to run a marathon, whether as a beginner or an improver, requires you to be healthy. I believe whether you run or not it's a wise move to have a yearly medical health check as a preventive measure. We all take it for granted, if we run a car, that it needs to go in for a service at least once a year, however people don't often demonstrate the same care and attention for themselves.

It seems that a lot of people take up running in their late thirties and early forties, worrying that they are getting out of shape and wanting to offset 'middle-age spread'. That is fantastic. In fact it is between the ages of 30 and 40 that most people put on at least 10 lbs in weight, which is carried as flab on the body. You may have been keen on sports and active in your teens, but that was 20 years ago, and you can't expect to have the same level of fitness now as you did then.

First, as already mentioned in the last chapter, you should consult your doctor if you:

are over 40
haven't exercised for over 10 years
have a sedentary lifestyle
are overweight
had an operation or serious illness in the last five years
have any known risk factors, such as diabetes, asthma or any heart trouble

The majority of people will have nothing to worry about and in fact will probably get a lot of encouragement from the doctor, seeing as vigorous exercise is known to reduce the risk of coronary heart disease.

If you have any risk factors it is a good idea to discuss them thoroughly with your doctor, because with good management and proper planning you may still be able to run.

On a day to day basis it is best not to run if you have a cough, a cold or 'flu, a tummy bug or a temperature. If you get a virus infection while training, although it may be difficult, give in and rest and get over it properly before returning to your programme. This may mean going back a week or two. But if you don't, you may end up prolonging the illness, which will then set you back even longer. Having had a break you will also find that you will enjoy your running all the more.

Diet

During this time of preparation it is worth having a look at your diet. To do this I suggest that you write down everything that you eat and drink, including alcohol, for a week. Make a note of everything, no matter how trivial – what you spread on toast, how much milk or sugar you have in tea and coffee, how many snacks, the lot.

What you are aiming to do is get a rough idea of what your diet is made up of and in what combination, i.e. carbohydrate (starches and sugars), proteins (animal or vegetable), fats (saturated or unsaturated) and alcohol.

At this stage I just want to consider the fat content of your diet. The Department of Health strongly recommends in their report[1] that we should aim to get less than 35 per cent of our energy from fat and less than half of that amount should be from saturated fat. At the same time as the report, the average person consumed about 42 per cent – nearly half – of their daily calories as fat.

We do need some fat in our diet – indeed, it is essential to life – but we only need a small amount to maintain good health. All this makes perfect sense for runners and in fact most serious runners will probably eat well below 30 per cent of their total calories as fat. Running is an endurance sport and although fat is a good source of energy, it metabolizes very slowly and therefore isn't the best fuel for running.

The proportion of the calories you derive from fat in your diet may come from 'hidden fats'. Just as this implies, such fat isn't noticeable, but is nevertheless there in cakes, biscuits, pastries, pies, sausages, crisps and nuts – all those lovely snack foods that are so easy to eat.

COMPARISON OF TWO DAYS' DIETS

A Conventional Day's Diet

BREAKFAST
fried sausage
fried bacon
fried eggs
fried bread
coffee with milk and sugar

LUNCH
chocolate bar
crisps
white cheese roll with butter
Coca-cola

DINNER
fish and chips
two slices of white bread and butter
two pints of beer

The energy consumed is about 1,500 cal, 50 per cent of which is fat, 33 per cent carbohydrate, 13 per cent protein and 4 per cent alcohol.

A Healthy Day's Diet

BREAKFAST
cereal/muesli with semi-skimmed milk
wholemeal toast and low-fat spread
honey
fruit/orange juice
tea with semi-skimmed milk

LUNCH
wholemeal ham salad sandwich with low-fat spread
apple
fruit juice/mineral water

DINNER
roast chicken
baked potato
cauliflower, cabbage, carrots
fruit salad and ice cream
a glass of wine

The energy consumed is about 1,000 cal, 21 per cent of which is fat, 60 per cent carbohydrate, 17 per cent protein and 2 per cent alcohol.

Having looked at your diet for a week and worked out approximately its fat content, you may want to make some changes. Try using low-fat alternatives such as low-fat spreads and semi-skimmed or skimmed milk. Replace Cheddar cheese with Edam, eat less red meat and more fish and poultry. Trim fat off all food and grill rather than fry. Replace snacks with fruit, vegetables and carbohydrate alternatives, such as bread, pasta, rice and potatoes.

Remember, eating is one of the pleasures of life and food can be tasty as well as healthy.

Resting Pulse

The speed of your pulse before and after exertion is a very good indicator of your overall fitness and is something that we can assess for ourselves quite easily. Heart rates vary from person to person; however, the fitter you are, the lower your heart rate will be at rest and the quicker it will return to its normal level after exertion.

Your resting pulse is the pulse you take first thing in the morning when you have just woken up. During your period of preparation take your pulse every morning and keep a record of it. As you get fitter you will notice how it gets slower – that is a good sign.

Experienced runners use this morning resting pulse rate as a useful check on the state of their health. If it is 10 per cent above normal, this is an indication that they may be succumbing to a bug or be overtired, and they will adjust their training accordingly.

Another way of gauging your fitness is to monitor your recovery rate, which is the time taken for your pulse to return to as close as possible to your normal rate after exercise. Take your pulse when you stop running, then at regular intervals of about five minutes while you go through your cool down routine, until you record a normal reading. As your fitness improves so the recovery rate decreases. Recovery time will also vary according to the intensity and duration of your training, so always compare like with like.

If you take a note of both of these measurements on a monthly basis you will notice your improved fitness.

BUPA Fitness Test: How Fit Are You Really?

Fitness Level	Beats per Minute at Rest			
Age	20–29 yrs	30–39 yrs	40–49 yrs	50+ yrs
Men				
Excellent	under 60	under 64	under 66	under 68
Good	60–69	64–71	66–73	68–75
Fair	70–85	72–87	74–89	76–91
Poor	over 85	over 87	over 89	over 91
Women				
Excellent	under 70	under 72	under 74	under 76
Good	70–77	72–79	74–81	76–83
Fair	78–94	80–96	88–92	84–100
Poor	over 94	over 96	over 98	over 100

Fitness Level	Beats per Minute after Exercise			
Age	20–29 yrs	30–39 yrs	40–49 yrs	50+ yrs
Men				
Excellent	under 76	under 80	under 82	under 84
Good	75–85	80–87	82–89	84–91
Fair	86–101	88–103	90–105	92–107
Poor	over 101	over 103	over 105	over 107
Women				
Excellent	under 86	under 88	under 90	under 92
Good	86–93	88–95	90–97	92–99
Fair	94–110	96–112	98–114	100–116
Poor	over 110	over 112	over 114	over 116

Information supplied by *The BUPA Manual of Fitness and Wellbeing*.

YOUR TARGET HEART RATE

In order to know how hard you need to work during training, you need to know your target heart rate. Getting your pulse as near as possible to this rate will make your heart more efficient and therefore fitter. To start with you may find it hard to work to this target, but as you get fitter it will be easier.

How to Calculate Target Heart Rate
Theoretical maximum pulse = 220 minus your age
Theoretical maximum pulse – resting pulse = pulse range
Pulse range – 2 + resting pulse = target heart rate in exercise

If you take a man of 40 with a resting pulse of 70, his target heart rate will be:

220 – 40 = 180
The pulse range is therefore between the resting pulse of 70 and the maximum of 180, a difference of 110.
Half of this difference of 110 is 55, which, added to the resting heart rate of 70, gives the target heart rate of 125 beats per minute.

Equipment

RUNNING SHOES

Let's start at the bottom, with what you wear on your feet. We are completely spoiled for choice today with the variety of running shoes that are on offer and in fact only about 15 per cent of shoes made are actually used in sporting activities. Your shoes will be the biggest expense that you have when it comes to running and it is worth getting it right. Although you want shoes that look good, never sacrifice comfort for style; they are not a fashion accessory, they have a job of work to do. If you get inadequate shoes, not only will you end up replacing them, but you will also run the risk of causing yourself injury.

Friends, family and other runners may have their opinion about the type of running shoe that will be right for you. Take their advice, but get yourself along to a specialist running shop.

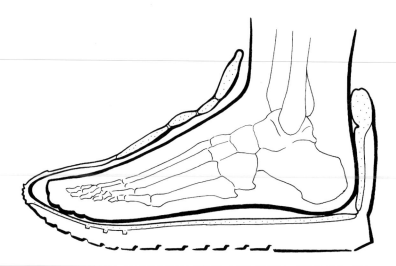

Once there, do not expect to do the deal in five minutes flat. If you have to try on 10 pairs of shoes before you find the right ones, so be it. Explain what you want the shoes for, the type of mileage you will be doing and the various surfaces you may be running on – road, grass and track. If possible, take an old pair of running shoes with you, as they will indicate the areas of wear specific to you. We all have individual feet, but shoe manufacturers have recognized three main areas of wear on the heel – neutral, pronator and superpronator – as well as other patterns of stress.

A good assistant will take into account your weight and height, and try and assess how hard you strike the ground as you run. Even if you are a complete beginner, he or she will still be able to assess your needs and offer you a range of footwear.

Let the assistant actually look at your feet – this will give a very good idea of the kind of shoes that will be comfortable for you. Try them on with the thickness of sock that you will train in. It will be a help to take along your own running socks or buy a pair there in order to make sure you get right fitting shoes. Also remember that you don't want the shoes to fit like a glove; when you run your feet will swell slightly and you will want a pair in a size that will allow for this. It may sound obvious, but try on both shoes and lace them up.

Pay particular attention to the depth of material on the heel of the shoe. This is the part that strikes the ground first with every footfall and it needs to offer enough cushioning to absorb the shock of most of the body's weight landing on a hard surface like the road. However you don't want the heel so thick that you feel as though you're falling forward and too thick a heel reduces the force exerted by the Achilles tendon on each stride. A heel with a thickness of about 2 cms (¾ in) will probably be most comfortable.

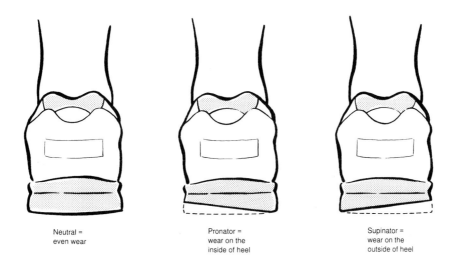

Neutral =
even wear

Pronator =
wear on the
inside of heel

Supinator =
wear on the
outside of heel

Look for a shoe that has plenty of material in the sole unit to provide good cushioning and flexibility. If you will be mainly road running, look for shoes made especially for the road, as they will have longer wearing soles with extra cushioning for the harder surface.

Some shoes have a raised heel tab, which is only there to help you to pull the shoe on. You will find that it digs into your Achilles tendon when running and be very irritating.

Check that you can't feel any rubbing from stitching in the shoe, particularly across the top of the arch of the foot, where there can be very inflexible, reinforced stitching. This will not soften with wear – but you'll only find that out after you've been putting the miles in.

You may want to think about safety when buying shoes and you will find many makes have reflectors stitched on to the body of the shoe.

Finally, when you are happy with a pair, if your budget will allow, buy two pairs. You will find a second pair invaluable in wet weather training; also, by the time you've broken a pair in, really like them and want to get another pair, you will often find that that style has been replaced.

It is recommended that you change running shoes at about 600 miles, depending on wear and tear, however I find I change after about 1,000 miles.

SOCKS

There are many varieties of sport socks on the market and although some people prefer to run without socks, they do offer protection between the shoe and the foot, reducing the risk of blisters and absorbing moisture. The best socks are all cotton or a cotton mix.

It's a wise investment to get a tub of vaseline, as it will help stop friction when applied between the toes and cut down the risk of blisters.

CLOTHING

If you look good then the chances are you will feel good, but once again, let comfort be your guide. Don't choose any clothes that will restrict your running, so nothing too tight, no tight waistbands, nothing that rubs. You can also feel uncomfortable in clothes that are too loose, bulky or heavy.

Of course, we all take to running in our own particular way and I am reminded of a story I heard about 15 years ago. It concerns a woman in her forties who was rather self-conscious about running. She didn't want to draw attention to herself or let her family in on what she was doing, so she would run in a hat and coat, and flat, sensible shoes, carrying a hand bag, as if she were running for a bus. It took her six months to pluck up the courage to put on a tracksuit and running shoes and let her family in on her secret!

Men and Women

Clothing for men and women is more or less the same, and what you wear will be down to your personal preference. Women will, however, need a jogging bra or a minimal bounce top and men will need shorts with in-built pants for support. Men may also benefit from the use of vaseline, as they can fall prone to 'jogger's nipple', which is a chafing of the nipple area caused by the friction between a sweaty top and the runner's body. In fact no race occurs without the runners' ritualistic smearing on of vaseline at all points of friction to alleviate future soreness!

Try to find clothing that will let the body 'breathe' when you run. In both hot and cold weather you can build up a lot of moisture, so use natural fabrics like cotton, or cotton and lycra mix, or fabric made into a mesh that will let the air pass freely through.

Summer Clothing

Running in the summer poses very few problems and all you need is a T-shirt or vest and a pair of shorts. You might want a sweat shirt for warming up and cooling down. Depending on how hot it is, you may also consider wearing a cap like a baseball hat, which will protect you from overhead sunshine as well as offering shade from the glare. You may find a sweat wrist-band useful and if running in the sun, always apply protective sun cream.

Winter Clothing

Running in the cold and wet weather of winter may require a few outfits. You can definitely overdress for warmth when you set out and regret it once the body's temperature rises, so it's worth putting up with the cold initially in order to run with less clothing at a comfortable temperature.

On the top half of your body wear layers of thin thermal clothing that will trap the body's heat. You will feel less bulky and can easily peel off a layer if you get too warm. Over these wear either a tracksuit top or a fleece, which is lightweight and really warm.

On the lower half of your body wear either tracksuit bottoms or running tights. Covering up the muscles in your legs in the winter is of great necessity in the prevention of strains and pulls.

You may wish to invest in a complete rain-suit or wetsuit for training in wet weather. You will find that it will offer protection against the wind and the rain, which is important for the serious runner.

Safety is important when you run, especially either at night or in the winter when the days are shorter and often the daytime visibility can be poor. A lot of sports clothing now comes with reflective tapes stitched on. Alternatively, you can buy reflective strips that can be attached at the wrists and ankles.

Last but not least, do not forget the extremities. You can lose up to 70 per cent of the body's heat from your head, so cover up with a woolly or thermal hat. Finally, there is nothing more truly miserable than going out on a run in the winter without gloves. Get some woolly or thermal gloves, with or without fingers, and if you get too warm, you can always put them in a pocket.

Most running clothes do have pockets, but I often find, especially in summer when I'm just wearing a top and shorts, that I don't have any. So I have got used to wearing a small lightweight bum bag, particularly on longer runs, to carry keys, a bit of change and perhaps a sweet or two.

OTHER EQUIPMENT

You will also need a watch with a stop-watch facility and serious runners will probably want to invest in a heart rate monitor, which can be bought at a good sports shop or through running magazines.

When to Run

Nobody can actually tell you when is the best time for you to run and you may discover that you have to vary your training according to the demands that work and family place on you. Elite athletes train twice a day and have a very finely tuned running programme, whereas beginners and improvers are looking to train once a day, with either one or two days' rest a week. Whenever you do choose to run, make sure you haven't eaten for at least two to three hours. Some people like to run first thing, while others prefer to run at the end of the day. It does help to run at a regular time, but don't be too inflexible if you need to accommodate some changes.

she runs....

The Running Club

Joining a club is a very good idea for a beginner and one way of finding a club is to ask at a local running shop. Some clubs are also listed in the local phone book and at the back of running magazines. You will find club members are very supportive of a new runner and you will soon fall in with others at your level. Running with people makes the whole experience a lot more enjoyable – you can compare notes and keep each other going.

If you feel nervous about joining a club, go along to a social evening, which usually occurs after a training session, where you can meet the members and ask any questions that concern you.

If you are a complete beginner, you may be advised to work towards being able to run comfortably for 30–40 minutes, and once you have attained that level, you will find running with a club a lot more beneficial and enjoyable. The previous chapter gives you a complete guide to starting from scratch.

You will probably find that you will run with a club once a week and you will find someone at a similar level whom you can run with at another time during the week. This is a great help as the mileage increases. Make sure, however, that unless you want to be pushed, you run at your own pace. It's very easy to fall in with people who know what they're doing, only to find that you are out of your depth. You can combine the sociability of a club with your own training schedule, as long as you are clear and stick to your guns.

The benefits of running with a club:

- **You have company and it makes running a lot easier.**
- **If you want to improve you can be encouraged to run faster by those who have experience.**
- **You have mental company to stave off boredom and you are stimulated to go out for a run because you are with other people.**

On a group basis a club will meet once or twice a week. A club local to me meets on a Wednesday evening; there will be 40–50 runners of assorted ability there, so a newcomer will always find someone at their level to run with. There is a staggered start, the slowest going off first, followed by a medium group and finally the fast group, all on the same route. The faster group will often go on and loop back, so doing a longer run in the same time. Some clubs have a women's night and at most clubs there is also a track night once a week which the faster runners attend to do specific interval training and speed work to improve their performance.

If you are going out at the weekend to do long runs you will probably meet up with other people from the club out for their run.

As already mentioned, it is advisable to be at the stage where you can run 30–40 minutes on your own comfortably before joining a club, but don't worry how fast you can run. If you approach a club and say that you can run 30–40 minutes but quite slowly, that will be alright and you will fit in.

Clubs don't necessarily have coaches, but there will be some very experienced runners there and the president or chairperson will deal with new members. He or she will ask you what level you run at and slot you into the most comfortable group. A club isn't about judging whether you are a good or bad runner, but about helping you in your running and building up your confidence, so they will take a realistic approach to what you can do.

If you have been accepted to run a marathon and approach a club, there will be help to get you through, but you may be encouraged to spend at least a year enjoying running, entering 10k races and building up to a half marathon before going into a marathon event.

One thing that often happens in a club is that quite a few people will be training for a particular marathon at one time and so you won't be on your own, there will be a lot of back-up to help you to focus on what you're doing and the miles won't be such a slog.

Clubs also organize a lot of fixtures. There will be a race nearly every Saturday throughout the year and in the summer, which is the road season, there will be the chance to do 10ks and half marathons. As well as their own club events, the club will also enter other fixtures, so if you want to race you can.

Some clubs will take on youngsters from the age of 10 or 11, but they are closely watched so that they don't burn out. Other clubs may only be for adults. In the last 20 years many more women have joined running clubs and proved to be very good runners.

When you join a club there will be a yearly subscription, which isn't usually a lot to pay, and most clubs will have premises and offer shower facilities.

In order to find out if a particular club is right for you, it is a good idea to try it out for a couple of weeks before paying a subscription. Don't get put off if one club doesn't work out – find another. A good club will have a happy blend of very good fast runners and all the rest who enjoy running and being part of a club, and no distinction will be made between the two groups, everyone will mix socially and pass on tips and share experiences.

It took me two marathons to pluck up the courage to join a running club and in consequence I missed out on a lot of help and fun – so, be brave and get along to a club sooner than later.

A running club can also help you with routes to run. Variety is all-important and you should aim to find at least half a dozen different routes, with a variety of surfaces, so your running isn't all on the road. Work out routes in parks, on towpaths, through woods and up and down hills. It's a good idea to run on a track occasionally; it's a measured distance and you can do some speed endurance work.

If you want to plan your own routes, drive around them in a car so as to measure the distance accurately. One thing you can't do is guess the distance. While training for a marathon last year, I fell in with another runner, a woman, and we started chatting. She told me she was doing a run that day of 12 miles and when I asked her the route, I realized that it was one often used by runners, but was actually only 9 miles. She had just guessed at the distance and I think had hoped it was 12 miles!

It is of great value to race over shorter distances through your training period and again this is where a club is of great use, providing you with information on upcoming races. Many races take place on a regular basis and if you are new to a club they will be able to let you know what events will occur in advance. You can then slot them into your programme and train accordingly.

Setting Goals and Targets

When you are preparing to run a marathon, whether for the first time or not, you need to work out how you are actually going to use your time. To choose the kind of training programme you need to follow, decide as best you can on the time you are aiming for in the marathon. You may find as the training progresses that you have over- or underestimated your time, but you can deal with that then.

BEGINNERS

As a beginner to running you may have no idea what sort of time you are aiming for, will be glad to 'just get round' and will be looking for at least a five-hour marathon. You will need to follow the beginners' programme in this book, which is a minimum of 24 weeks. If you have longer to prepare, all the better, but a normally healthy person should be able to do the distance in this time, if keeping to the programme. Remember, you are entering an endurance event and the longer the body has to get used to the demands, the better.

IMPROVERS

You may be someone who runs to keep fit and covers about 25 miles a week. Your body is already used to the activity and having decided to take on a marathon, you will be building on your fitness with a training programme aiming to complete a sub four-hour race. You may not have followed a training programme before and the schedule for improvers will take you through a 16-week training period. If you have longer than 16 weeks, you may want to spend time repeating the earlier weeks.

Depending on the period of time that you give yourself overall to train, break it down into blocks of months and weeks, and work out a specific aim for each block.

What you are aiming to do by organizing your time in these blocks is to train in the most appropriate and enjoyable way for your level, and to set attainable goals during the training which will keep you focused and motivated. The best training for running is running. Once you know what you're aiming for with your running you can determine your training programme, and as you are training, you need a record of how you are getting along.

KEEP A RUNNING DIARY

As you can see in Liz's account of running *(see pp.121–128)*, she has been keeping a diary of her training and racing since she was 11 years old. This was something she did for herself quite naturally. Perhaps she had an inkling that she would excel in her field and wanted to keep a record of how it all came about. However, all élite athletes are encouraged to keep a diary of their training and their racing. This also happens to be a very useful tip for all runners, no matter what level.

Once you have worked out your goals in the long-term, i.e. the marathon, and the short-term, i.e. the training programme you are going to follow, you can transfer this information to your diary so that you can see each week and each month exactly what you are working towards, then daily you record the details of your training as it happens. To an extent, the diary can become another running companion.

This specific and personal account of your training will be a true record of how you are actually proceeding and will encourage you when the going gets tough, as it inevitably will. You can spot times when you made really good progress and try and work out what made the difference. You will also see how fatigue and the odd cold affect your training. If you vary your routes and the surfaces you run on, you will notice the difference in training and how you responded to the different conditions. As you approach races you can record your specific preparation. That will be of help the next time you race. So a diary has a very practical application, as well as being a psychological support.

You can use a real diary that you set aside for running or improvise and use an ordinary notepad, set out as follows:

Monday

(Date)............................Time...........................Distance/Time.......................................

Weather.........................Route...

Comments [i.e., did you run alone, with the club or anyone else; how did you feel, any aches or pains; did anything change throughout the run, did you speed up or slow down, did you need to drink?]

You see it's quite easy. You will probably also find that you will develop your own code for making notes. As an example, here's a section of my running diary leading up to London '96:

Sat 24 Feb:	Rest today – prepare for race tomorrow. Weather looks changeable. Did some stretching and yoga.
Sun 25 Feb:	½m Roding Valley. Poured with rain, but I got used to that. Took Isostar drink with me. Ran 1:48:36 – not too bad.
Mon 26 Feb:	3 miles in Richmond very slowly: 27:01. Very sunny and bright. Quads felt sore today. Could have gone on longer 'cos the slow pace felt comfortable.
Tues 27 Feb:	7 miles from home 57:46. Fastest over this distance to date, don't know how – quads still hurt, but I feel positive after the race on Sunday. Lovely spring day.
Wed 28 Feb:	9 miles 1:11:42. All four bridges Hammersmith–Kew. Not too slow but seem to be keeping up a bit of pressure.
Thurs 29 Feb:	6.2 in 48:00:45. This is weird – a week of PBs over my usual distances. Weather helps – having a run of blue crisp spring days. Steady 8 min miling is what I'm trying to maintain.
Fri 1 March:	Rest – cold grey day. Had a massage – sorted out the legs.
Sat 2 March:	12 miles – all four bridges from home. 1:36:26 – taking 9 minutes off the last time I did this distance. Felt easy and comfortable all through.

Total: 40.3 miles

SUMMING UP

- If you have any doubts or worries concerning your health, consult your doctor.
- Spend some time in choosing the right footwear. If possible buy two pairs of running shoes.
- Depending on the time of year, sort out the appropriate clothing.
- Get a watch with a stop-watch facility.
- Decide the time you are aiming for in the marathon and choose which training programme to follow.
- Decide on the period of time involved and break it down into blocks of months and weeks. Make a note of the specific aims for each block.
- Join a club and let them know that you are training for a marathon.
- As soon as you choose to run any races, fit them into your training programme.
- Start a running diary.
- Work out a variety of routes, with a variety of surfaces, including hills.

1 Report of the Committee on Medical Aspects of Food Policy: *Diet and Cardiovascular Disease* (1984)

five warm up and cool down

warming up the muscles and loosening the joints is very important before a training session. It is equally important to stretch the muscles or 'cool down' at the end of a session. This will soon become a very natural process as you feel the benefits, but in the beginning it may feel odd, especially if you are only running for a short time. You will, however, soon be increasing the time/distance, and warming up is vital in preventing injury and building up flexibility, so the sooner you get into good habits the better.

Consider, for example, that your muscles are 'cold' before you start – you may have just got up or been sitting for most of the day. The following set of exercises is specifically aimed at 'warming up' the various groups of muscles you will be using when you run, so running is easier and more comfortable and you will perform better.

When you run, you are aiming, at whatever level you perform, to be as efficient as possible, and developing the flexibility in the hips can make you a smoother runner with a good natural stride, so working on the hips before and after a run is necessary.

Doing a series of stretches after a run, once the muscles are well worked out, is a way of increasing their flexibility, as well as working out the metabolic waste products that are left in the muscles as a result of effort. It is these waste products that are the cause of stiffness, and stretching will ensure that you are less stiff the following day. To start with it may feel as though you will never feel anything but permanently stiff and sore, but that will pass, particularly if you build stretching into your training programme.

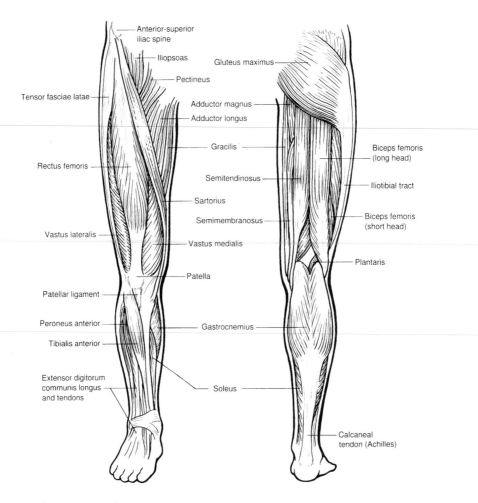

Anterior-superior iliac spine

Iliopsoas

Gluteus maximus

Pectineus

Tensor fasciae latae

Adductor magnus

Adductor longus

Gracilis

Biceps femoris (long head)

Rectus femoris

Semitendinosus

Iliotibial tract

Sartorius

Semimembranosus

Biceps femoris (short head)

Vastus lateralis

Vastus medialis

Plantaris

Patella

Patellar ligament

Peroneus anterior

Gastrocnemius

Tibialis anterior

Extensor digitorum communis longus and tendons

Soleus

Calcaneal tendon (Achilles)

The muscular system of the legs.

Warming Up

Warming up increases the flow of blood through the soft tissues, widening the blood vessels in and around them. Their temperature rises so they become more supple and elastic – ready for work.

You will notice as you train in different weather conditions that warming up is particularly important in the winter months, when the muscles are shorter by virtue of the fact that it is cold.

Your warm up routine is of psychological benefit, too. When you go to races and it all seems new and strange, just getting on with your tried and tested routine has a very levelling and grounding effect, which can help dispel anxiety.

When you do the warm up routine, do not jerk or bounce, but let the exercise be a slow sustained effort, using the weight of the body naturally and breathing easily. If you feel stiff or sore from your last training session, go easy to start with, as the muscles wake up. Let pain be your guide. Don't continue to warm up if you are in pain.

As we get older, the body, without any exercise, becomes less mobile and less flexible. If you are a beginner at running and you have been leading a sedentary lifestyle, to just set out running can be damaging. You might actually feel alright on the run, but if you intend sticking to a training programme over a sustained period of time, where the workload will get harder, give yourself every chance, and prepare yourself through warming up and cooling down regularly.

GENERAL LOOSENING EXERCISES

These exercises are to be done before the warm up.

Upper Body Twisting

Standing with the feet apart and parallel, facing forward, raise the arms to shoulder height, forming a 'T' shape. Swing the arms freely to the right, then left, twisting at the waist. Repeat this 16 times.

Side Stretch

With feet hip width apart and parallel, place your left hand on your left hip, reaching upwards and over with your right arm, feeling the stretch all down the right side. Squeeze your bottom so that your hips stay in line. Alternate stretches from right to left eight times.

WARM UP EXERCISES

You may require a support for some of these exercises – such as a wall, door, tree or another runner!

Quadriceps Stretch (front of thigh)

Standing on the left leg, keeping knees together, pick up the right ankle in the right hand. Gently pull the right heel back towards your bottom, stretching the muscles in the front of the thigh. Hold for 30 seconds and repeat on the other leg.

Extended Quadriceps Stretch (optional)

Standing on the left leg, pick up the right foot by the toes and pull the leg outwards and backwards. You will feel a deeper stretch in the front thigh muscles as well as in the groin. Hold this position for 30 seconds then change legs.

Achilles Tendon and Lower Calf Stretch

Stand as far away from your support as you can so that when you lean on it you feel the stretch up the back of both legs. Once in the leaning position, step forward with the left leg, keeping both feet flat and the right leg straight out behind you. You will feel the stretch in the Achilles tendon and lower calf of the straight leg. Hold for 30 seconds and repeat on the other side.

Achilles and
Calf Stretch (optional)

Lean forward with the hands and feet flat on
the ground forming a triangle shape. Lift the
right foot and lock it behind the left ankle,
feeling the stretch in the Achilles tendon and
calf muscles of the left leg. Hold for 30
seconds and repeat on the other leg.

Hamstring Stretch
(back of thigh)

Standing with the feet together, roll the top of
the body forwards, breathing out as you do so.
Take hold of the ankles or wherever you can
reach, keeping the shoulders relaxed and
breathing easily. You will feel the stretch in the
muscles at the back of the leg, running from
the knee to the bottom. Hold this position for
30 seconds and slowly come back to standing.

Adductor Stretch (inner thigh)

Squat down on the right toe, with the left leg out to the side, resting on the heel. Finding your balance, hold the left toes in the left hand and gently pull the foot back towards you, stretching the muscles on the inner thigh between the knee and the groin. Hold this for 30 seconds and change sides.

Whole Leg Stretch

Lunge forward on the left leg, stretching the right leg out behind you and supporting your weight on the left knee. Feel the stretch in the hamstrings and gluteus maximus (bottom) on the left side, and in the quadriceps and hip flexors (front of groin) on the right side. Hold this for 30 seconds and repeat on the other side.

Whole Outside Leg and Abductor Stretch

Standing with feet together, cross the right foot over the left foot, keeping ankles and knees close together. Roll the upper body forwards, twisting towards the inside left foot, feeling the stretch along the outside left leg. Hold this position for 30 seconds and change legs.

Adductor and Groin Stretch

Standing with the feet wide apart and spread slightly outwards, hands on hips, slowly lower the upper body about 6–8 inches (15–20 cm), making sure the knees always bend directly over the feet. Feel the stretch along the inner thigh and in the groin. Hold for 30 seconds and come back to standing.

Cooling Down

It is almost as bad for your body to stop abruptly after exercise as it is to set off suddenly without warming up. Cooling down allows the hard-working blood vessels to shut down gradually and so prevent blood pooling, which can cause a sudden drop in blood pressure. That is one of the reasons some people faint after hard exercise.

Remember, muscles tighten and joints get less mobile as you get older, so even if you have been running for years, keep up the stretching routine and perhaps increase it slightly by repeating a few of the exercises you find especially beneficial, particularly those for the hips.

If you are warming up outdoors before a run, make sure that you keep warm during the session, although you may discard a layer when you set off. Similarly, when you've finished your run and you're quite warm, cover up again to maintain your body temperature while doing the cool down exercises.

COOL DOWN EXERCISES

Repeat three or four of the warm up exercises for quads, hamstrings, Achilles and calves, and add one or two of the following to release tension in the upper body.

You will find the body more responsive to stretching after a run as there is a good supply of blood to the muscles. The cool down routine is insurance against injury; it builds up flexibility and strength.

Shoulder Release

Standing with feet together, stretch the left arm across the body at shoulder height, palm facing backwards. Bring the right arm up underneath and lock elbows together. Pull the left arm gently by the right arm, feeling the left shoulder release. Hold for 30 seconds and change sides.

Arm and Neck Release

Take the left arm under and behind your back, bringing the right arm over your shoulder so that the fingers of each hand meet in the middle of your back. Grasp the fingers together and pull, feeling the stretch in the neck and both arms. Hold for 30 seconds and repeat on the other side.

Abductor Stretch and Lower Back Twist

Sitting on the floor, both legs straight out in front, lift the right leg and cross it over the left leg, placing the right foot alongside the left calf. Support your weight on your right hand behind you and bring the left arm across the body, using the elbow as a lever on the right knee. Gently exert pressure from the elbow onto the knee, so stretching the outer thigh muscles of the right leg and releasing tension in the lower back. Hold for 30 seconds and repeat on the other leg.

The three following exercises are from the discipline of yoga and I have found them particularly beneficial, especially after a long run.

The pictures show the end position of each exercise, which is reached through several stages.

Wide Leg Stretch/Prasarita Padottanasana

Stand on a non-slip surface with your feet as far apart as possible, feet facing forward and hands on hips. Lean back slightly, then slowly bending forward, slide the hands as far down the legs as they will go. If you can, stretch out from the spine, placing the hands on the floor. You will feel the stretch in both legs and in the hips. Breathing easily, hold the position for 20 seconds and slowly come back to standing.

Triangle/Triconasana

Standing with feet about a metre apart, right foot turned out, left foot forward, place the hands on the hips, body facing forward. Slide the right hand down the body, feeling the stretch along the left side. Slide the hand right down to the ankle, keeping the shoulders open. Raise the left arm, palm facing outwards, and hold the position for 20 seconds. You will feel the stretch through the whole body, toning the leg muscles and improving the strength and flexibility in the hips. Hold the position for 20 seconds and repeat the other side.

The Cat

Kneel on all fours with legs slightly apart, hands at shoulder width. Raise the head as you breathe in and hollow or dip the spine. As you breathe out, tuck the chin into the chest and round the spine as much as you can. Slowly alternate these two movements six times, feeling the stretch and releasing tension in the whole spine.

Liz's kinesiologist has devised a specific set of exercises to warm up the different muscle groups while placing the least stress possible on the lower back and joints. For some of them she uses a length of rope to give her extra leverage and resistance.

Quadriceps Stretch

Lying on the left side, loop the left arm behind the left knee. Take hold of the right ankle with the right hand, pulling the heel back towards the bottom. This levering position gives a thorough stretch to the front right thigh. Hold the position for 30 seconds and repeat on the other side.

Hamstrings/Gluteal/Lower Back Stretch

Lying on your back, raise the left knee towards the armpit, holding behind the knee with the right hand while keeping the back flat on the floor. Holding the left foot with the left hand, gently pull the left knee closer to the body, feeling the stretch in the hamstrings, up through the gluteal (bottom) muscles and deep into the lower back. Hold for 30 seconds and change legs.

Anterior Tibialis (front of shin) and Achilles Stretch

Sitting on the floor, right leg relaxed, bend the left knee, bringing the left heel alongside the right knee. Grasp the toes and pull them back towards the shin, feeling the stretch in the left Achilles and all up along the front of the left shin. Hold for 30 seconds and repeat on the other leg.

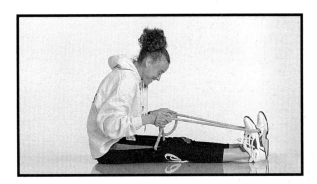

Calf Stretch with Rope

Sitting on the floor with your legs straight out in front, loop a rope around the sole of the right foot and, keeping that leg straight, pull on the rope, so stretching the calf muscles in the right leg. Hold this for 30 seconds and change to the other side.

Whole Leg Stretch with Rope

Lying on the floor, loop the rope around the sole of the left foot, keeping the right leg relaxed and the back flat on the floor. Straighten the left leg out and slowly draw it towards the body, stretching the calves, hamstrings and gluteal muscles. Hold the position for 30 seconds and change legs.

LIZ:'One of the things that has been introduced into my pro- gramme is a half-hour work-out that I do twice a week. I do a circuit of nine exercises for upper body strength using low weights with high repeats – going from one to the other with no recovery. I complete the session with three small circuits of sit- ups, star jumps and bounding – the last two are great for the feet and ankles.'

This type of routine may be something that you might want to include in your training. However it is very intense and should only be included once or twice a week. The aim is to strengthen your body to improve your running performance – you don't want to be too bulky, but you do want what you've got to work to the best of its ability. Fit the work-out into your schedule on an easy day, but not a rest day.

If you are not sure what exercise to do, seek advice from a gym. If you don't belong to one, you can often get day membership and if you explain to an instructor what you want specifically, he or she will be able to help you. Alternatively, if you have joined a running club, you will find help from other runners.

SUMMING UP

■ Always do your warm up routine to wake up the muscles, loosen joints and increase the blood circulation. Keep covered up while warming up.

■ Cool down after a run – you may need to walk for a while, especially after a long run, so the body isn't shocked suddenly by stopping.

■ Do slow sustained stretches to lessen stiffness.

■ If you want to increase overall body strength or upper body strength, incorporate one or two circuits of exercises that can be done at home or a gym. It's good to get advice on these from an instructor.

six types of training

when you start a training schedule with your goal of running a marathon, there are various methods of training that combined will give you a very sound foundation and lead to a successful run.

Long Slow Distance Running

It goes without saying that in order to be able to run distance, you have to be able to run distances. It is therefore important that you get used to doing a long run once a week, with a slightly less long run midweek. This is an easy paced run, at a slower pace than you anticipate your race pace to be. The aim of this kind of running is to slowly build up your strength and stamina endurance.

Joe Henderson, a prolific writer on the subject of running, brought out a book called *Long Slow Distance: The humane way to train* (Anderson World Publishing, 1969). He wanted to emphasize the enjoyment that can be gained by 'casual, gentle, lighthearted running'. Long slow distance – LSD – means running long distances steadily at a slower than race pace so that you finish your runs feeling good and wanting to do more. For example, if you are an eight-minute miler, you slow your pace down to nine or ten minutes per mile or even slower. Those of you who run regularly will be aware of your minute per mile pace, but if you don't know what your pace is, just get along to a park with a measured track distance and time yourself. Alternatively you can drive a mile distance and time yourself over that.

LSD running in this way has many benefits, as it builds up stamina and aerobic capacity, develops muscle, burns fat and reduces the risk of injury. It is also an approach that can be used by new runners of all ages.

For a fun runner this type of training is ideal; however, there are several types of training that, combined with the easy paced running, will significantly improve your performance, and these are incorporated into the schedules for both beginners and improvers.

Pace Running

Running at race pace is an important part of your preparation in distance running and you should aim to do at least one session a week at race pace.

In a pace session don't aim to run flat out, but run faster than you do in an LSD session. Therefore as an example if your pace in the easy paced LSD session is nine or ten minutes per mile, come up to your race pace of eight minutes. You are aiming to run at about 75 per cent of your effort. For beginners who are running to set times, try to clock your time at specific places along your various runs. When you do a pace run, aim to arrive at each place sooner each run. Effectively, you will be covering more distance in less time.

Hard Fast Running

This type of training is included from the start of the training schedules for both beginners and improvers. As the description implies, you are dramatically increasing your pace over a short distance so that you are running flat out. It needs to be a fast sustained effort at whatever level you can manage for 15–20 minutes. Having thoroughly warmed up, run at an easy pace for five minutes and then up the pace to hard fast running for 15–20 minutes, after which it is best not to stop immediately, but run slowly for a further five minutes before your cooling down routine.

This is a version of the type of speed endurance work that Liz and Eamonn do, and it is this work that pays off for them in their terrific results. Having excelled in the 10k distance, they have made a natural progression to the marathon distance. Their training hasn't changed that much, except that now they obviously regularly incorporate long runs. Good short distance training and racing improves their marathon performance – and in the speed endurance work they aim to push themselves to run faster than their race pace over a short controlled distance, with the result that their race pace feels natural and comfortable.

Interval Training

This is only suggested for improvers, as it is a very effective method of training to increase your race pace. The work is often done at a track, but can be done anywhere on a flat level surface.

At this level try 6 x 2 minutes hard running with a five minute recovery jog between each effort. If beginners want to try it, run for two minutes and do a very slow jog for five minutes, six times.

The aim is to push yourself to near maximum effort so that your heart rate is about 180–200 beats per minute, then recover with slow jogging so that the heart rate drops to about 120 bpm, before pushing yourself for another hard effort.

As you push yourself to the limit in these short controlled bursts you are training your body to experience fatigue and the need to get oxygen to the working muscles as quickly as they can. This is called 'repaying the oxygen debt'. You are training your heart and lungs to become more efficient.

Fartlek

This is a Swedish form of training and a direct translation of the word is 'speedplay'. The idea is to break up the usual routine of a session and to incorporate all sorts of activities such as jogging, walking and running at a variety of speeds.

A child at play will happily sprint, skip, walk, jog and run in no particular order; a fartlek session aims to introduce these natural and carefree forms of movement into a training session.

One way to do this for yourself is to incorporate a 20-minute fartlek session into an easy run session. Use handy markers like trees, lamp posts and pillar boxes as start and stop points, and vary your pace and activity as much as you can, from flat-out hard fast running to brisk walking.

Training like this can be very beneficial in breaking up the monotony of your sessions. On a practical level, it is also a way of changing pace within a session, which is vital in distance running. There are moments during the marathon when you get locked into your pace and to just vary it for 100 metres or yards can be refreshing, stave off cramp and keep you on course.

Racing

You will notice in the training schedules for both beginners and improvers it is suggested that instead of a long run on a Sunday, you compete in a race. It may not always be convenient to fit these in strictly according to the programme, but do make every effort to do at least one 10k race and one half marathon at about the time specified. If you have raced before, you will be competing against your personal best and know that by bringing down your 10k time you can affect your overall marathon time. For most runners the aim is to place yourself under race conditions and see how you react. These early races are part of your preparation for the marathon itself. You want to get round the course as steadily and comfortably as you can.

Races are advertised in running magazines and at sports shops. You will learn most comprehensively about fixtures through a running club. The sooner you slot races into your schedule the better, preparing yourself both mentally and physically for what's ahead.

Tips for Racing

- Decide what you will wear – which will inevitably depend on the weather. Do not break in new shoes at a race.
- Get to the race with plenty of time to spare.
- Don't leave anything valuable in your kit.
- Warm up before the race as you would normally do before a run. If there is a delay, keep warm by jogging or cover up with a tracksuit or a bin-bag.
- Time yourself with your own watch for accuracy.
- Attempt to run at least the first five miles at your own race pace – don't run with the crowd.
- If you get into difficulties, keep moving, even if you slow right down to a walk. Only stop if you are in pain.
- Don't race if you are unwell, feel that you have a cold or bug coming on, or are not properly recovered from an injury.
- At organized races there will be drink stations. However you may wish to take a water bottle or isotonic pouch with you.

SUMMING UP

- Practise LSD running on the long Sunday runs.
- Plan a variety of routes so that when doing a pace run or a hard fast run you have a consistently level surface for at least 20 minutes/two to three miles.
- Improvers: Plan where you can do interval training – if not at a track, a sports field is ideal.
- If you don't want to do a complete fartlek session, incorporate different speeds and styles into a planned run as part of a warm up or cool down routine.
- Slot races into your schedule as soon as you can and use your diary to record your preparation, results and comments.

seven 16-week schedule
for beginners and improvers

Unless specified, all runs are at an easy pace – long slow distance (LSD).
(For the various training methods, see the previous chapter, pp.60–64.)

16 WEEKS TO GO

	Beginners	Improvers
Mon	20 mins	5 miles
Tue	25 mins pace	5 miles hard fast
Wed	20 mins	7 miles
Thur	30 mins hard fast	5 miles pace
Fri	rest	rest
Sat	30 mins	4 miles
Sun	40 mins	8 miles
Total	**2 hrs 45 mins**	**34 miles**

15 WEEKS TO GO

Mon	25 mins	5 miles
Tue	35 mins pace	7 miles hard fast
Wed	30 mins	5 miles
Thur	30 mins hard fast	6 miles pace
Fri	rest	rest
Sat	35 mins	4 miles
Sun	40 mins	8 miles
Total	**3 hrs 15 mins**	**35 miles**

14 WEEKS TO GO

Mon	30 mins	5 miles
Tue	40 mins pace	7 miles hard fast
Wed	30 mins	7 miles
Thur	30 mins hard fast	5 miles
Fri	rest	rest
Sat	45 mins	4 miles
Sun	55 mins	8 miles
Total	**3 hrs 50 mins**	**36 miles**

13 WEEKS TO GO

Mon	40 mins	5 miles
Tue	rest	6 miles hard fast
Wed	45 mins pace	8 miles
Thur	50 mins	6 miles pace
Fri	rest	rest
Sat	50 mins	5 miles
Sun	60 mins	8 miles
Total	**4 hrs 05 mins**	**38 miles**

12 WEEKS TO GO

The beginners' schedule is increasing in time, maintaining the pace and hard fast runs twice a week.

The improvers' schedule also includes intervals of fartlek training as well as the pace and hard fast runs. You may find, once you include these forms of training into your programme, that you will be more tired, so get plenty of rest.

Both groups are encouraged to enter races during these next four weeks, but don't race against the clock unless you are experienced. Use the races to try out your preparation for racing and to get used to running in a crowd of strangers. Aim to get round as steadily and comfortably as you can.

Mon	40 mins	5 miles
Tue	45 mins pace	6 miles hard fast
Wed	35 mins	8 miles pace
Thur	40 mins hard fast	5 miles int/fartlek
Fri	rest	rest
Sat	45 mins	6 miles
Sun	60 mins	10 miles
Total	**4 hrs 25 mins**	**40 miles**

11 WEEKS TO GO

Mon	45 mins	5 miles
Tue	55 mins pace	5 miles hard fast
Wed	40 mins	8 miles pace
Thur	45 mins hard fast	5 miles int/fartlek
Fri	rest	rest
Sat	45 mins	6 miles
Sun	65 mins	12 miles or 10k race
Total	**4 hrs 55 mins**	**41 miles**

10 WEEKS TO GO

Mon	45 mins	5 miles
Tue	60 mins pace	6 miles hard fast
Wed	40 mins	8 miles pace
Thur	55 mins hard fast	6 miles int/fartlek
Fri	rest	rest
Sat	45 mins	5 miles
Sun	70 mins or 10k race	10 miles or 10k race
Total	**5 hrs 15 mins**	**40 miles**

9 WEEKS TO GO

Mon	35 mins	6 miles
Tue	45 mins	5 miles hard fast
Wed	55 mins	8 miles pace
Thur	45 mins hard fast	6 miles int/fartlek
Fri	rest	8 miles/rest
Sat	50 mins	rest/8 miles
Sun	75 mins	13 miles or ½ marathon
Total	**5 hrs 05 mins**	**46 miles**

8 WEEKS TO GO

Times and distances are still increasing, with the combination of the various methods of training. Improvers may have already run a half marathon by now and both groups are encouraged to include a half marathon in their training over the next four weeks. Use any notes made in your diary from the last race to help you prepare and read the section on racing *(p.62)*.

Mon	40 mins	5 miles
Tue	60 mins pace	6 miles hard fast
Wed	40 mins	8 miles pace
Thur	60 mins hard fast	5 miles int/fartlek
Fri	rest	rest
Sat	40 mins	8 miles
Sun	85 mins	15 miles
Total	**5 hrs 25 mins**	**47 miles**

The women's start on the 1992 Great North Run.

7 WEEKS TO GO

Mon	40 mins	5 miles
Tue	60 mins pace	5 miles hard fast
Wed	30 mins	8 miles pace
Thur	60 mins hard fast	6 miles int/fartlek
Fri	rest	rest
Sat	40 mins	10 miles
Sun	100 mins	15 miles
Total	**5 hrs 30 mins**	**49 miles**

6 WEEKS TO GO

Mon	40 mins	5 miles
Tue	80 mins pace	6 miles hard fast
Wed	40 mins	8 miles pace
Thur	75 mins hard fast	5 miles int/fartlek
Fri	rest	rest
Sat	40 mins	10 miles
Sun	120 mins or ½ marathon	15 miles or ½ marathon
Total	**6 hrs 35 mins**	**49 miles**

5 WEEKS TO GO

Mon	20 mins	5 miles
Tue	40 mins pace	5 miles hard fast
Wed	30 mins	8 miles pace
Thur	90 mins hard fast	5 miles int/fartlek
Fri	rest	rest
Sat	40 mins	10 miles
Sun	130 mins	18 miles
Total	**5 hrs 50 mins**	**51 miles**

4 WEEKS TO GO

The end is in sight! This last period of preparation and training is crucial. You will now be feeling comfortable covering the longer distances. If you hit any low moments, get that diary out and remind yourself how far you've come. This can prove a testing time, as 'race anxiety' creeps in. Take each run as it comes, aim to do your best and study all the advice for the last four weeks (see pp.109–111).

Mon	35 mins	5 miles
Tue	70 mins pace	5 miles hard fast
Wed	40 mins	10 miles pace
Thur	rest	6 miles int/fartlek
Fri	50 mins hard fast	5 miles
Sat	rest	rest
Sun	150 mins	19–21 miles or 20 miles race
Total	**5 hrs 45 mins**	**50–52 miles**

3 WEEKS TO GO

Mon	20 mins	3 miles
Tue	40 mins pace	6 miles hard fast
Wed	30 mins	12 miles
Thur	70 mins hard fast	8 miles int/fartlek
Fri	rest	rest
Sat	30 mins	5 miles
Sun	120 mins	15 miles
Total	**5 hrs 10 mins**	**49 miles**

2 WEEKS TO GO

Mon	20 mins	3 miles
Tue	40 mins pace	6 miles hard fast
Wed	30 mins	12 miles pace
Thur	70 mins hard fast	5 miles int/fartlek
Fri	rest	rest
Sat	40 mins	6 miles
Sun	100 mins	12 miles
Total	**5 hrs**	**44 miles**

LAST WEEK

Mon	30 mins	5 miles
Tue	rest	5 miles/rest
Wed	25 mins	4 miles
Thur	rest	3 miles
Fri	10 min jog	rest
Sat	10 min jog/rest	10 min jog/rest
Sun	26.2 miles	26.2 miles

Pace Chart

1 mile Pace	5 miles	10 km (6.2 m)	15 km (9.3 m)	10 miles	20 km (12.4 m)	Half-Marathon (13.1 m)	15 miles	25 km (15.5 m)	30 km (18.6 m)	20 miles	40 km (24.8 m)	Full Marathon
4.45	23:45	29:27	44:11	47:30	58:54	1:02:16	1:11:15	1:13:38	1:28:21	1:35:00	1:57:48	2:04:33
4.50	24:10			48:20			1:12:30			1:36:40		2:07.44
5.00	25:00	31:00	46:30	50:00	1:02:00	1:05:33	1:15:00	1:17:30	1:33:00	1:40:00	2:04:00	2:11:06
5.10	25:50			51:40			1:17:30			1:43:20		2:15:28
5.15	26:15	32:33	48:50	52:30	1:05:06	1:08:50	1:18:45	1:21:23	1:37:39	1:45:00	2:10:12	2:17:40
5.20	26:40			53:20			1:20:00			1:46:50		2:19:50
5.30	27:30	34:06	51:09	55:00	1:08:12	1:12:07	1:22:30	1:25:15	1:42:18	1:50:00	2:16:24	2:24:12
5.40	28:20			56:40			1:25:00			1:53:20		2:28:34
5.45	28:45	35:39	53:29	57:30	1:11:18	1:15:23	1:26:15	1:29:08	1:46:57	1:55:00	2:22:36	2:30:16
5.50	29:10			58:20			1:27:30			1:56:40		2:32:56
6.00	30:00	37:12	55:48	1:00:00	1:14:24	1:18:39	1:30:00	1:33:00	1:51:36	2:00:00	2:28:48	2:37:19
6.10	30:50			1:01:40			1:32:30			2:03:20		2:41:41
6.15	31:15	38:45	58:08	1:02:30	1:17:30	1:21:56	1:33:45	1:36:53	1:55:45	2:05:00	2:35:00	2:43:53
6.20	31:40			1:03:20			1:35:00			2:06:40		2:46:03
6.30	32:30	40:18	1:00:27	1:05:00	1:20:36	1:25:13	1:37:30	1:40:45	2:00:44	2:10:00	2:41:12	2:50:25
6.40	33:20			1:06:40			1:40:00			2:13:20		2:54:47
6.45	33:45	41:51	1:02:47	1:07:30	1:23:42	1:28:29	1:41:15	1:44:38	2:05:33	2:15:00	2:47:24	2:56:59
6.50	34:10			1:08:20			1:42:30			2:16:40		2:59:09
7.00	35:00	43:24	1:05:06	1:10:00	1:26:50	1:31:46	1:45:00	1:48:30	2:10:12	2:20:00	2:53:40	3:03:33
7.10	35:50			1:11:40			1:47:30			2:23:20		3:07:55
7.15	36:15	44:57	1:07:26	1:12:30	1:29:54	1:35:03	1:48:45	1:52:23	2:14:51	2:25:00	2:59:48	3:10:06
7.20	36:40			1:13:20			1:50:00			2:26:40		3:12:17
7.30	37:30	46:30	1:09:45	1:15:00	1:33:00	1:38:19	1:52:30	1:56:15	2:19:20	2:30:00	3:06:00	3:16:39
7.40	38:20			1:16:40			1:55:00			2:33:20		3:21:01
7.45	38:45	48:03	1:12:05	1:17:30	1:36:06	1:41:36	1:56:15	2:00:08	2:24:09	2:35:00	3:12:12	3:23:13
7.50	39:10			1:18:20			1:57:30			2:36:40		3:25:23
8.00	40:00	49:36	1:14:24	1:20:00	1:39:12	1:44:53	2:00:00	2:04:00	2:28:48	2:40:00	3:18:24	3:29:45
8.10	40:50			1:21:40			2:02:30			2:43:20		3:34:07
8.15	41:15	51:09	1:16:44	1:22:30	1:42:12	1:48:10	2:03:45	2:07:53	2:33:27	2:45:00	3:24:24	3:36:20
8.20	41:40			1:23:20			2:05:00			2:46:40		3:38:29
8.30	42:30	52:42	1:19:03	1:25:00	1:45:24	1:51:26	2:07:30	2:11:45	2:38:06	2:50:00	3:30:48	3:42:51
8.40	43:20			1:26:40			2:10:00			2:53:20		3:47:13
8.45	43:45	54:15	1:21:23	1:27:30	1:48:30	1:54:43	2:11:15	2:15:38	2:42:45	2:55:00	3:37:00	3:49:26
8.50	44:10			1:28:20			2:12:30			2:56:40		3:51:35
9.00	45:00	55:48	1:23:42	1:30:00	1:51:36	1:57:59	2:15:00	2:19:30	2:47:24	3:00:00	3:43:12	3:56:00
9.10	45:50			1:31:40			2:17:30			3:03:20		4:00:22
9.15	46:15	57:21	1:26:02	1:32:30	1:54:42	2:01:16	2:18:45	2:23:23	2:52:03	3:05:00	3:49:24	4:02:32
9.20	46:40			1:33:20			2:20:00			3:06:40		4:04:44
9.30	47:30	58:54	1:28:21	1:35:00	1:57:48	2:04:33	2:22:30	2:27:15	2:56:42	3:10:00	3:55:36	4:09:06
9.40	48:20			1:36:40			2:25:00			3:13:20		4:13:28
9.45	48:45	1:00:27	1:30:41	1:37:30	2:00:54	2:07:49	2:26:15	2:31:08	3:01:21	3:15:00	4:01:48	4:15:33
9.50	49:10			1:38:20			2:27:30			3:16:40		4:17:50
10.00	50:00	1:02:00	1:33:00	1:40:00	2:04:00	2:11:06	2:30:00	2:35:00	3:06:00	3:20:00	4:08:00	4:22:13

eight eating and running

getting the most out of your running depends on several factors: putting in the right amount of physical effort and fuelling that effort with a balanced, healthy diet.

We have already talked about fat in the diet and suggested some changes that could be made, now let's take a look at your whole diet and how what you eat can produce the energy required for your optimum performance in running.

First and foremost, we need food to supply the body with the energy required to sustain life. About 70 per cent of the energy we derive from our food is used in the maintenance of our essential processes, such as keeping the heart pumping and the liver and kidneys functioning, etc. That means the remaining 30 per cent is the energy used in all our external activities such as working, driving, gardening or exercising.

All sorts of food appeals to us for a variety of reasons, but when it comes down to what the body needs, it can be considered in terms of how much energy is released when the food is burned up by the body cells. The amount of energy in food depends on how much water, carbohydrate, protein and fat it contains.

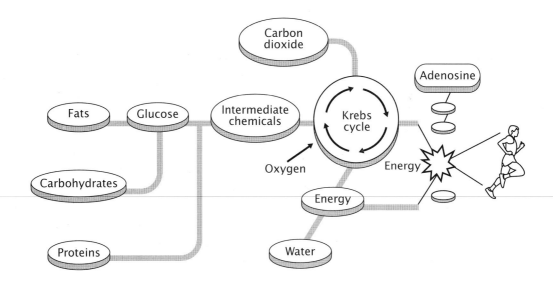

In the Krebs cycle, energy from glucose and, when glucose is not available, from other carbohydrates, fats and proteins is converted into chemical form capable of rebonding phosphates and re-forming molecules of ATP (adenosine triphosphate). As a result of the chemical reactions of the cycle, the waste products carbon dioxide and water are formed, which are then eliminated from the body through the lungs.

On a daily basis the body strives to keep a balance between energy intake and output. If you burn more energy than you eat, you will notice a weight loss and if you eat more than you burn, you will notice a weight gain.

Energy is measured as calories, however the correct term is 'kilocalorie', which scientifically means the amount of heat needed to warm up a litre of water to one degree. The amount of calories required for each individual daily depends on many factors, such as age, height, shape, lifestyle and heredity.

A healthy diet is one that not only keeps all your basic processes functioning, but also protects you from a range of chronic conditions like coronary heart disease, adult onset diabetes, bowel cancer and high blood pressure.

If you are going to add the workload of a marathon training programme to your life, you will be looking to fuel that activity from what you eat. You will want to build and maintain muscles, increase stamina and endurance to sustain the effort of running over many hours. You don't need to follow a 'faddy' diet whatsoever to be able to run, but you may find that you will want to make subtle changes so that you are eating food that gives you longer sustained energy.

Let's take a look at the various components that make up our diet and see how good they are at giving us that energy.

Carbohydrate

Carbohydrates are a group of complex compounds consisting of carbon, hydrogen and oxygen and include both sugars and starches.

Sugars are known as 'simple carbohydrates' and supply the body with energy and no other nutrients. Examples of these include sugar (sucrose), glucose, honey, syrup, jams and marmalade, sweets and chocolate.

Starches are known as 'complex carbohydrates' and the best exist in the natural unrefined state. They contain starch as well as vitamins, minerals and fibre. Examples include bread, pasta, rice, porridge, potatoes, bananas, apples and dried fruit.

When carbohydrate is broken down in the body, it is stored as glycogen in the liver and in the muscles. Glycogen is the most readily available and efficient source of energy used in any vigorous activity such as running.

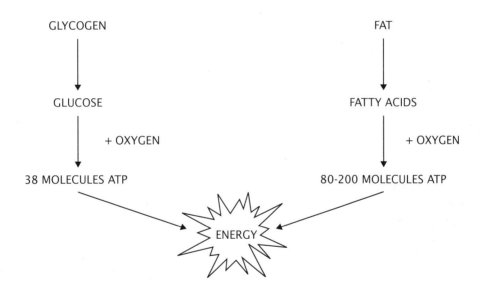

It has long been thought that carbohydrate was the fattening food in a diet, however research has shown that a diet high in carbohydrate is essential to producing energy for any sustained activity, so you may find that you will want to slightly increase your intake of carbohydrate.

It is best to go easy on the sugary high-carbohydrates, such as cakes, pastries, pies and biscuits, however, as these highly processed foods have little in the way of vitamins, minerals and fibre, but often a lot of fat. But eat as many of the more nutritious, complex, starchy carbohydrates as you need.

Fat

The building blocks that make up fat are called 'fatty acids', and depending on their structure they are either saturated or unsaturated. Fats that are solid at room temperature, like butter and lard, are high in saturated fat and are mostly built up from saturated fatty acid units. Most saturated fats are found in animal and dairy products.

The other building blocks, the unsaturated fatty acids, are liquid at room temperature and can vary between the most unsaturated – polyunsaturated – and least unsaturated – monounsaturated. Oils usually have a high level of polyunsaturated fatty acids.

Fats from plant sources like nuts and olives are generally less saturated, but two plant oils, coconut and palm oil, are highly saturated.

Foods higher in saturated fat	Foods lower in saturated fat
butter, margarine, lard, suet	margarines (high in polyunsaturates), low-fat spreads
'cooking oil' (unspecified), coconut and palm oil	corn oil, olive oil, sunflower oil and safflower oil
beef, lamb, pork, bacon, ham, duck	chicken (no skin) fish, shellfish
meat pies, pastries, sausages, pâté, salami	llow-fat alternatives
whole milk, cream, Cheddar cheese, Edam	semi-skimmed or skimmed milk, Brie, cottage cheese
crisps, mayonnaise, peanut butter, cakes, biscuits	fruit and vegetables, pasta, rice, potatoes, wholegrain cereals

Cholesterol

Cholesterol is a fatty substance present in all mammals and is an essential constituent of cell membranes. We can both absorb it and make it. There are carefully regulated processes in the body which ensure that the level of cholesterol never gets too low. In fact the level we have when we are born is adequate and is about a quarter of what we have subsequently, so most of us have an unnecessarily high level. Research has shown that a raised level of blood cholesterol is associated with a higher risk of having a heart attack in later life. If we eat the wrong sorts of foods we may increase our blood cholesterol level. These include foods such as dairy products and red meat that are high in saturated fat. In processing these dietary fats the liver seems encouraged to pour out large levels of cholesterol.

Cholesterol is carried around the bloodstream by proteins called 'lipoproteins'. The two main types are high density lipoprotein (HDL) and low density lipoprotein (LDL). HDLs are known to have a beneficial effect and protect against the risk of coronary heart disease, by carrying fat away from the heart to the liver to be disposed of, while the more harmful LDLs carry most of the cholesterol around the body. The aim is to increase the ratio of HDL to LDL. It is known that sustained vigorous activity raises the levels of HDL, as does moderate amounts of alcohol.

When you run you increase the activity of the enzyme lipoprotein lipase, which is present in skeletal muscle, heart muscle and adipose (fat) tissue. The more of this enzyme you have, the more effective you will be in breaking down the fat molecules (triglycerides), thus lowering your LDLs and raising your HDLs. Studies have shown that runners do indeed have high HDLs and low LDLs.

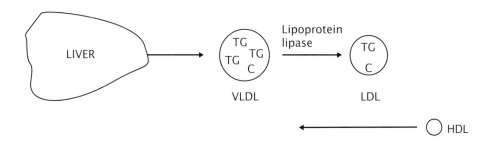

TG = Triglyceride
C = Cholesterol
VLDL = Very low density lipoprotein
LDL = Low density lipoprotein   } 'Bad' cholesterol
HDL = High density lipoprotein: 'Good' cholesterol

Protein

About 17 per cent of our body tissue is made up of protein, and we derive it from two sources: animal and vegetable. Protein is used to form muscle and organ tissue, is present in bones, skin, hair and nails, and is seen more as a building material rather than an energy store. It is considered that we normally eat more protein than is needed, particularly animal protein, and few people in the Western world will suffer from a deficiency.

All proteins are made up of a combination of chemical components known as amino acids. Most of these are made in the body, but eight of them have to be provided from the diet.

Animal sources of protein include meat, poultry, offal, fish, shellfish, milk, cheese, yoghurt and eggs. This source of protein may be high in fat, so you may want to consider adding more vegetable protein to your diet.

Vegetable sources of protein include legumes, lentils, peas, beans (e.g. haricot, mung, butter beans and baked beans), nuts and seeds, bread, potatoes, pasta and rice. This source of protein is also high in carbohydrate and fibre.

The daily recommended amount of protein for endurance athletes is 1.2–1.4 g (0.05 oz) per kg (2.2 lb) body weight per day. So a 70 kg (11 stone) person would require 48–98 g (1.6–3.2 oz) of protein a day. You may find that this is slightly lower than your normal intake, but this is the weight of protein with little or no fat and is sufficient to maintain a healthy active lifestyle.

Water

Water is one of the most important nutrients required by the body, performs many vital functions and is about 60 per cent of our total body weight. It is used to transport other nutrients and metabolic waste products around the body, and plays an important part in regulating the body's temperature through sweating. This is of great importance during exercise.

Water is derived from most of the food that we eat as well as from the fluids that we drink. We normally lose about 2 litres (4 pints) of water a day and so we need to replace at least that.

> **LIZ:** 'I think people underestimate the role water plays in a runner's diet. Of course you have to get the nutritional balance right, however I believe water is a very important part of achieving that balance. To a beginner it may feel odd to drink two or more litres a day, but if you spread it out you'll not notice it. I carry water with me all the time and take sips all the while. As a runner you should never be thirsty.'

Vitamins and Minerals

Vitamins and minerals are chemical compounds that are needed by the body in tiny amounts for specific bodily functions. Because these nutrients are so important to our health, we have to eat a range of food to supply us with what we need, and although we in the West have a wide range of food on offer, deficiencies can occur. To counteract this, it is possible to take vitamin and mineral supplements, and many runners feel that because they are putting their body through a lot of stress, these supplements will help their body maintenance and ward off infection.

> **LIZ:** 'I take a multi-vitamin every day and a 25 mg chelated iron supplement. I think the iron is particularly necessary for women. It also helps with fatigue.'

It is true that inadequate iron can affect the strength and endurance of runners, and this results in what's known as 'sports anaemia'. Some women may suffer from a lack of iron due to menstruation and so benefit from the supplement. Iron is best taken if it is chelated for optimum absorption and utilization, and in combination with vitamin C, found in citrus fruits, orange juice and berries. Some iron supplements include vitamin C.

If you feel that you require a supplement to your diet, it is advisable to consult either your doctor or pharmacist first.

Fibre

Fibre is the non-digestible outer layers of plants and seeds. As it doesn't actually supply the body with energy, it is sometimes overlooked in its nutritional importance. There are two types of fibre: soluble and non-soluble.

Soluble fibre, such as oats, sweetcorn and kidney beans, can be partially digested, and is thought to help in lowering blood cholesterol by combining with it and then leaving the body as waste product.

Insoluble fibre passes through the body without being digested and is essential to the proper functioning of the gut.

Sufficient fibre in the diet will help prevent such conditions as constipation, bowel cancer and gallstones. Any increase in fibre should be accompanied by an increase in water, as the fibre absorbs a lot of water as it passes through the body.

Alcohol

Alcohol, which is derived from fermenting carbohydrate with yeast, is a source of energy. The difference between the energy from alcohol and the energy from sources like carbohydrate and fat is that alcohol cannot supply the muscles with energy needed in exercise. Any energy you do derive from alcohol will be stored by the body as fat and an excess of alcohol can damage your liver.

The current guidelines issued by the Government are that men should not drink in excess of 28 units of alcohol per week and women should not drink in excess of 21. A unit of alcohol is half a pint of beer, a small glass of wine and a single measure of spirits.

Elite runners in training will drastically reduce their intake of alcohol, if not cut it out completely, primarily because it is so dehydrating. Fun runners need not be so abstemious, and by keeping well within the guidelines and maintaining your other fluid levels, your running shouldn't be impaired.

Putting It All Together

No matter how much you enjoy running, it should be more important to be healthy. Fortunately, a healthy balanced diet is just what you need to improve your performance as a runner.

The World Health Organization has published guidelines in its document *Diet, Nutrition and the Prevention of Chronic Diseases*, which advises the following:

55 per cent of our energy to be derived from carbohydrate
10–15 per cent of our energy to be derived from protein
30 per cent of our energy to be derived from fat

I would suggest a slight adjustment to these figures and would aim for:

60 per cent carbohydrate
15 per cent protein
25 per cent fat

If about 60 per cent of your diet is made up of carbohydrate and you eat 2,000 calories a day, you'll want to eat about 300 g (12 oz) carbohydrate, and if you eat 3,000 calories a day, you'll want to eat about 450 g (18 oz) carbohydrate.

Once you start training you will want to be gradually increasing your calorie intake by approximately 100 cals for men and 75 cals for women for every mile run. Here is an example of ways to put this into practice.

Breakfast:	Cereal/muesli and wholemeal toast, fresh fruit/orange juice. Tea with semi-skimmed milk.
Lunch:	Sandwiches with a filling of your choice on wholemeal bread and salad. Jacket potatoes, 'chunky' vegetable soup with wholemeal bread.
Dinner:	Pasta or rice dishes, with not too fatty a sauce. Accompany meat dishes with potatoes, vegetables and salads. Incorporate pulses, nuts and beans into meals.
Snacks:	Fruit, dried fruit, salads, crispbreads, oatcakes, low-fat spreads and dips, and cereal fruit bars.

Of course lunch and dinner are interchangeable if you prefer a larger meal earlier in the day.

EATING OUT

If you are out and about, there are a lot of takeaway foods available. Out of these try to choose those with the least fat. Opt for chicken or fish burgers, for example, instead of beef burgers. Pizza and pasta are good choices, as are baked potatoes instead of chips.

Chinese and Indian food is high in carbohydrate, with lots of vegetables, noodles and rice. Try to combine these dishes with a non-meat choice occasionally.

You can see that with a bit of thought you really can put a diet together that will satisfy your taste buds and keep you healthy as well as supply you with the right sort of energy for running.

When I started to increase my mileage one thing that I noticed about my eating pattern was that my weight seemed to stabilize for the first time in many years. I had been on all sorts of diets for at least 20 years, without much success. However, running sorted all that out. I need to burn up a certain amount of energy a day and running is my way of doing that. Then I can eat just what I want, knowing it will be used up, not just turn to fat. Because of the running I began to feel really hungry, food tasted fantastic and I found that I ate just what I needed, no more or less. I had found the point where I wanted to stop.

I have spent a lot of time thinking about diet and health. Because of my lifestyle, I was either a 'boredom' eater, hanging around a TV studio and grazing all day, or a 'comfort' eater, working away from home and filling myself up when I wasn't hungry, just to have that full and happy feeling inside. So I stopped dieting, started running, and my whole system seemed to quite naturally and gently sort itself out. I truly believe a little of what you fancy does you good, but the operative word is 'little'. That way you can eat a whole range of food and be healthy and happy. If you couple that attitude to food with your commitment to a running programme, you'll have a very dynamic combination. There'll be no stopping you!

Vegetarians and Running

Many people have decided to make changes to their diet these days and the term 'vegetarian' may need defining:

> **Semi- or demi-vegetarians are those who have cut out all forms of red meat, but still eat poultry and fish.**
> **Lacto-ovo vegetarians are those who have cut out all forms of meat and fish, but eat animal products such as cheese, milk and eggs.**
> **Vegans are those who have cut out all animal products.**

There is absolutely no reason why someone who follows a vegetarian diet shouldn't run as well as a meat eater. However there are several dietary components that vegetarians need to be aware of to maintain a healthy balanced diet: protein, iron, calcium and vitamin B_{12}. Sources of these are given below.

It is generally thought that protein can only be derived from an animal source, an idea which we have seen to be inaccurate. There are eight amino acids that we require from our diet and these can easily be supplied to a vegetarian. Combining certain foods such as beans, pulses, nuts and cereals is also an excellent way of ensuring a healthy protein intake.

> *Vegetarian sources of protein:* **Dairy products, eggs, soya milk, tofu and quorn.**
> *Vegetarian combinations for protein:* **Beans on toast, peanut butter sandwiches, vegetable and lentil curry with rice, macaroni cheese, humus and pitta bread, porridge made with milk.**
> *Vegetarian sources of iron:* **Wholegrains such as oats, wheat and rye; all nuts; bread and soya products; dark green leafy vegetables such as spinach, watercress and broccoli; potatoes. Black strap molasses; sun-dried raisins. (Vitamin C aids the absorption of iron so it's a good idea to include citrus fruits, orange juice and berries with these meals.)**
> *Vegetarian sources of calcium:* **Milk, yoghurt and cheese, fortified soya milk, wholemeal bread, spinach, nuts, seeds, tofu and pulses.**
> *Vegetarian sources of B_{12}:* **Eggs, milk, soya milk, yeast extract, wheatgerm, fortified breakfast cereal.**

Generally, vegetarians are very aware of their diet and are quite health conscious. As they eat no meat products, there is less fat in the diet and a lot more carbohydrate and fibre – which is just the healthy combination that runners need. If you are a vegetarian in training for a marathon, remember that you will need to increase your food intake gradually by approximately 100 calories for every mile run.

The Best Energy Source for Running

Studies were carried out in Sweden over 50 years ago to discover the importance of carbohydrate in the performance of vigorous exercise.

Those taking part were asked to pedal a stationary cycle at a constant rate and with a normal diet were able to cycle for about two hours before exhaustion set in. They were then fed a diet high in carbohydrate for a couple of days and repeated the test; they could cycle for nearly twice as long. A couple of days later, after a diet very low in carbohydrate, they could only cycle for one to one and a half hours. From this it was concluded that carbohydrate has a significant effect on those who take part in endurance activities.

GLYCOGEN – THE RUNNER'S FUEL

The energy needed for you to run – glycogen – is made from glucose, which is the result of carbohydrate digestion. Glycogen is stored in your muscles and liver. The more glycogen you have, the longer and harder you can run. However there is only a finite amount of glycogen the body can store, so in an endurance sport like marathon running, one of the benefits of the training is that the body also derives energy from the fat deposited just beneath the skin. It is this mixture of energy from carbohydrate and fat that enables you to prolong the important glycogen stores. This is why most experienced runners are thin – their bodies have become more efficient at converting this mixture of energy, in order to economize on the precious glycogen stores.

When you do a training session, you run down your level of glycogen. If you were to go out the next day and expect to do the same session without replacing the loss, you would notice a very real difference in what you could do. You would still be able to train on a low level of glycogen, but the body adapts to the amount of energy available, so you would be considerably slower and fatigue would set in a lot sooner.

If you start a training session with low glycogen levels, you will not perform well and there will be little improvement. This really affects morale. It's one thing to know you are tired and so decide to have an easy run, but if you want to push yourself and haven't actually got the energy to do it, you can feel very frustrated and demoralized.

So, you need to fuel yourself to get the most out of your training. The amount of glycogen you use depends on what you are doing in your training session; you will need more glycogen for a 15-mile run than for a five-mile run at the same pace. However, you might need more for a fast paced five-mile run than for a slow, easy 15-mile run.

The body actually has to learn to refuel between training sessions and an experienced runner will carry out this process more quickly than a beginner, which is why in the beginning, not having got the balance right, you might feel sluggish and slow. Your body is learning to use your energy store for a new activity. The good news is that it doesn't take too long for the body to make these adjustments.

Bearing in mind that the best time to run is between two and three hours after a meal, the best time to refuel is immediately after a run. It is in the first two hours after a run that the body is most efficient at making and storing glycogen. You may not feel like a full meal then, but a high carbohydrate drink or snack will do to start with; bananas are an excellent easily digestible energy source, as tennis players demonstrate.

It is considered that the most efficient eating pattern to maintain glycogen levels is 'little and often'. This doesn't mean five full blown meals a day, but five light, carbohydrate based meals. The reason for this is that the body works at a fixed rate in converting glucose into glycogen and will convert nearly all the carbohydrate from a small meal into glycogen. However, if you concentrate all of your carbohydrate in one huge meal, the body, still working at this same fixed rate, will store as much glycogen as it can, the rest being stored as fat.

I found that eating 'little and often' really suits me, as it supplies me with constant energy and I don't have that stuffed, bloated feeling you can get after one huge meal. I also find that I eat when I'm hungry rather than because it's time to, which is a very natural rhythm. However, I know this is not practical for everyone, and eating three meals a day, with the emphasis on plenty of fresh fruit, vegetables and carbohydrate with less fatty food at each meal, is a healthy, balanced way to eat.

Fluid and Running

As already mentioned, 60 per cent of the body is made up of water and in normal conditions we lose about 2 litres/4 pints a day through the body's processes. If we do not replace this fluid, we can be considered dehydrated.

When you run, your muscles start to produce extra heat and you will feel quite warm as a result. To function healthily, the body needs to remain at a constant temperature between 37–38°C/98–100°F. The body copes with this rise in temperature by sweating, as water evaporates from the surface of your skin, causing you to lose heat. During hard or prolonged running, especially in hot or humid weather conditions, it is possible to lose up to 2 litres/4 pints an hour. Losing this amount of fluid when running will seriously impair your performance, as well as place a massive strain on your whole system. Varying degrees of dehydration result in nausea, vomiting, diarrhoea, dizziness, difficulty in breathing and eventual collapse through heat stroke.

It is a very good idea to get into good habits when it comes to drinking. As it is natural to lose water when you run, make sure that you are as hydrated as possible before you run, by sipping all day. In fact you really cannot take on too much water.

As already mentioned, a good aim is to drink at least 2 litres/4 pints of water a day. This may seem an excessive amount to some, but you are probably a lot more dehydrated than you think. Tea and coffee have a diuretic effect, so you lose water through elimination. Working and living in either air conditioned or centrally heated atmospheres also slowly dehydrate the body. One way of telling if you are dehydrated is by the colour of your urine: it should be diluted and a weak pale straw colour. If it is dark yellow, you need to drink more water. Feeling thirsty is not a good indicator of dehydration, because when you know you are thirsty, it is too late. Avoid getting to that stage by sipping water constantly.

You can also take on more fluid when you are running but you may have to be patient while you develop your technique. At first there seems to be water everywhere except in your mouth! Some very experienced runners will actually stop to drink.

You don't have to worry about drinking on a run up to about 30 minutes, but on anything over that try and drink every 15 minutes.

Large volumes of fluid will be easily absorbed into the system, moving quickly from the stomach to the intestine. However this may make you feel very uncomfortable and you may prefer to take smaller amounts. The colder the drink, the quicker it passes through the system.

CARBOHYDRATE AND ELECTROLYTE DRINKS

There are a whole range of drinks on the market that are aimed at people performing in sport and contain different concentrations of carbohydrate and electrolytes. There may be some advantage to using these drinks in an endurance activity like running – the carbohydrate can give you extra fuel when reserves are dwindling, and the electrolyte can replace the salts lost through sweating and also boost absorption of water into the intestines.

If the drink is made up of particles more concentrated than the body's fluids it is called 'hypertonic'. It uses water from the body to dilute it and so absorption is slow. It may boost energy reserves. These drinks contain more carbohydrate in the form of glucose and sugar.

If the drink is made up of particles less concentrated than the body's fluids it is called 'hypotonic' and will be absorbed rapidly by the body.

If the drink is made up of particles of the same concentration as the body's fluids, they will be absorbed at the same speed as water.

The best advice with these various drinks is to try them out and see what works for you, as choice depends on length and intensity of running, and external factors such as temperature and humidity. If in any doubt, always drink water.

After running, start drinking immediately, in order to start the process of rehydration.

Dieting

A quick word here about dieting. Although medical experts advise combining exercise with a healthy diet as a means of losing weight, I do not recommend using a marathon training programme as a means of losing weight. I strongly feel that if you are putting your body under the pressure of a marathon training programme, you shouldn't be restricting the amount of calories you are eating, as they are your source of energy, and apart from anything else, you could make yourself ill.

I have suggested the best ways to supply that energy through a healthy diet and making slight adjustments to the way you usually eat. If you follow these, you may notice a slight weight loss over a period of time, at which point your weight will then stabilize.

If you feel that you need to lose some weight, I would suggest that you aim to do that first with a moderate exercise programme, such as the new runner's schedule, then think about running a marathon. You need to make a commitment to both activities and if you try to do both at the same time, chances are you will end up doing neither.

Loss of weight is quite normal during a marathon training programme. However, if you are at all concerned about weight loss, consult your doctor.

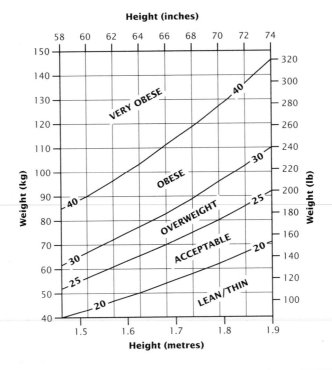

Height (inches)

Chart axes: Weight (kg) on left, Weight (lb) on right; Height (metres) along bottom. Categories: VERY OBESE, OBESE, OVERWEIGHT, ACCEPTABLE, LEAN/THIN.

Height (metres)

SUMMING UP

- Consider the changes, if any, you want to make to your diet.
- Tell your family, friends and work-mates that you are making these changes and ask them to help you. You may want to introduce a high-carbohydrate diet at home; it is a balanced and healthy way to eat for all the family.
- Keep a watch out for the foods you nibble as snacks. Cut out the high-fat foods like crisps, salted nuts, cakes, pastries and biscuits.
- Try out the occasional meal without meat.
- Replace red meat meals with fish and chicken.
- Take a note of your fluid intake per day and start including a lot more water, at least 1 litre/2 pints and if possible 2 litres/4 pints.
- If you drink alcohol, match the amount with the equivalent soft drink or water. Try to cut out spirits. Don't have a heavy drinking session the night before a long run or hard training run.
- On runs over 30 mins/5 miles make sure you are adequately hydrated. Learn to drink while you run.
- Always drink immediately after a run and start the glycogen refuelling as soon after a run as possible, with food or a high-carbohydrate drink.

Viking spirit to the fore on the Great North Run.

The feelgood factor.

Is this a bridge too far? Runners beating the traffic in the 1993 New York Marathon.

Top right Queen of the road – Liz sails home to victory at the '96 Flora London Marathon.

Top centre It's raining medals – what it's all about.

Above Time weighs heavily on the mind and everywhere else as these competitors find their final burst of energy.

Right Chariots of fire. The Wheelchair London Marathon is organized by BSAD – the British Sports Association for the Disabled. David Holding, a bookkeeper from Kettering, won the '96 London for the third time over a period of eight years in 1:43:48 and the women's race was won by Tanni Grey in 2:10.

Top left Water works. They may be opponents but they're in it together. Liz McColgan and Manuela Manchado share a drink on the 1995 BUPA Great North Run.

Bottom left Afterglow. Their smiles say it all. Mexican Dominicio Ceron celebrates his third consecutive London win and Liz McColgan shares that feeling with her first win on home ground.

Left Eamonn Martin deals with the hard shoulder – going on to win his debut marathon in London in 1993.

Sunshine Superman.

nine body maintenance

■ a man goes to his doctor and says, 'Doctor, it hurts every time I do that,'
raising his arm, and the doctor says, 'Don't do it then.' ■

Tommy Cooper

That's pretty useless advice to a committed runner – you know, injury permitting,
there is no way he or she is not going to run. We have had a look at what you put in
to your body to get the most out of it. We are now going to look at ways of maintaining the body through your training schedule and how to cope with any injuries that
may occur.

Causes of Injuries

INADEQUATE CLOTHING

One of the most common causes of injury is poorly fitting or badly made shoes.
It cannot be overstated that you really need to spend time on getting the right
shoes for you. If you buy them from a reputable dealer and they are a high
mileage shoe, for the surface you will be predominantly running on, you should
have no trouble.

Also, wear the appropriate clothing for the weather, especially in cold weather, as muscles take longer to warm up and need help to maintain that temperature.

INADEQUATE WARM UP

Another cause of injury is inadequate or no warm up. You know, if you oversleep in the morning and have to do everything in a mad rush, that it feels like lunchtime before you wake up. Running without preparing the body is the same. It is in a state of shock and will not perform well. You will also risk pulls and strains, as the muscles, joints and ligaments are not ready for the work they are being asked to do. So, whether you are running for 15 minutes or 15 miles, always warm up, particularly in cold weather. After your run, cool down with a series of stretches that will balance and strengthen your muscles. This will help you to feel less stiff and sore later.

TOO MUCH TOO SOON

Injury can also be caused by doing too much too soon. You will see from the schedules that there is a staggered approach to the increase in time or distance. Pushing yourself too soon can result in injury, if your body is not ready for it. Of course you mustn't be too cautious, but by following the structure of the programme you will move gradually through the pain barriers and be surprised at your achievement.

I remember the first time I ran what I called 'double figures'. The idea of going beyond 10 miles loomed up in front of me and I really didn't think that the day would come when I could do it. But I stuck to my training schedule and one day, I just knew I was ready. Off I went, alone, did 11 miles and really enjoyed it. I had been slowly increasing the miles so I wanted to do it, my diet was helping me, I took a drink with me to top up and the weather was wintry, but crisp and bright – it felt like an occasion. I won't deny there have been times since then that that distance has felt like a slog, but I have the good memory of that run to keep me going.

FATIGUE

One final factor that can cause injury is inadequate rest or recovery. When you are running, every session you are looking for improvement, whether it's in the distance you run, or the speed, or your running style. But before you attempt further improvement, you need to recharge your batteries by eating the right foods, drinking enough fluid and getting enough sleep. It has been suggested that if you train for distance running you will in fact need at least an extra hour's sleep a night.

Fatigue may not seem like an injury, but it can have a detrimental effect on your performance. Fatigue takes its toll on all runners. Sometimes it's just temporary, the result of having a difficult day. However, if you are overtraining, or not properly recovered from an illness or injury, fatigue can manifest itself in irritability, inability to sleep and perhaps diarrhoea. These are signals from the body to ease up and have a rest. You will be surprised to find that you won't lose fitness as a result and will return to running with renewed vigour.

Overtraining is as much a pitfall as not training enough and a good aim is to do the least amount of training to bring about the most improvement, which means that you do quality training, something that Liz now adheres to.

> **LIZ: 'I've made my mistakes by not resting and pounding on, putting in the miles, which means you run yourself down, and get things like colds and 'flu, or worse – injury. I do things differently now and work for quality in my training.'**

Rest is often overlooked by some top athletes who get a real buzz out of training and they need firm handling by their coach. If you are a beginner, you won't need to be told twice – you'll probably have already dozed off on the sofa! Your body knows just what it needs, so listen to it.

Symptoms that show you are overtraining are:

- **reduced appetite**
- **difficulty sleeping**
- **constant fatigue**
- **waking up tired and listless**
- **unplanned loss of weight**
- **recurrent infections and minor injuries**
- **irritability and mood swings**

CONDITIONS THAT MAY DEVELOP DUE TO RUNNING

Distance running can cause a condition called 'runner's haematuria', which is urine that is cloudy or has blood in it. This can clear up on its own, but if you're worried, consult your doctor.

Training extensively in hot weather can result in heat exhaustion and heat stroke – which can be fatal. These conditions can be prevented by taking sufficient fluids and covering your head. To deal with someone affected by the heat, get him or her into the shade and give him plenty to drink. If this doesn't bring relief, get him to a doctor.

Intensive endurance training can affect women, causing the pituitary gland to produce fewer hormones which control the menstrual cycle. This seems to occur when the percentage of body fat to body weight becomes very low. Periods may stop completely – this is called 'amenorrhoea' – but will return naturally with less hard training and an increase in body fat. If they don't return, or you notice any other changes in your menstrual cycle, consult your doctor.

You will probably have heard of 'runner's diarrhoea', or 'runner's trots', which may be the stuff of jokes, but is no joke to deal with. This is a form of colitis brought on because blood is diverted from the digestive tract to your muscles during long training sessions. Easing up on the mileage for a couple of days should bring relief. Remember that you become dehydrated with diarrhoea, so keep the fluids topped up.

Dealing with Injury

One thing you can be sure of when a group of runners get together is that they will all have a tale or two to tell about their injuries. What does become clear is that runners do become 'in tune' with their bodies, and are generally a fit and healthy breed.

One of the grey areas in the treatment of injury is how long to spend in recovery before running again, as different people respond differently to treatment.

Always take advice from your doctor or other medical practitioner, don't run with pain and build up gradually when you do start to run again. You will soon recover the lost ground, the rest will have done you good and you will be hungry to run.

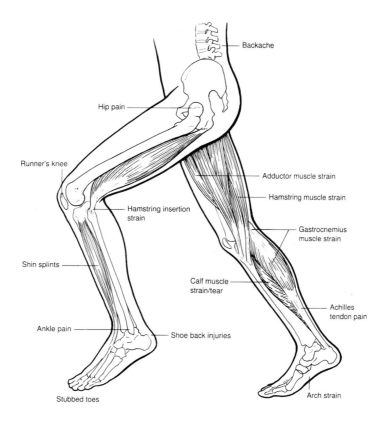

Runners' injuries.

Runners' injuries are mainly concentrated in the lower leg, so let's take a look at all the specific areas where injury occurs and why.

FEET

There are a range of niggling problems that can occur with the feet. Blisters are an obvious one and can be very painful, making running very uncomfortable. First of all make sure that they are not caused by ill-fitting or rubbing shoes. I used to get blisters on the end of both of my second toes, because they are longer than my big toes, a common condition called 'Morton's foot'. Having enough space for your toes to move freely can solve it. Sometimes running shoes shrink when they dry out, which can cause blisters, so pad out the toe of your wet shoes with newspaper to help them to retain their shape when drying.

People vary in their treatment of blisters. Some pierce the skin with a sterilized needle, drain out the fluid, clean the whole area with antiseptic and cover with a plaster. Others prefer to let them go down and just cover them with a plaster.

As to prevention, vaseline is good protection against blisters, spread liberally over the particular area. Alternatively, soak the feet in a black tea (this is a dancer's trick). Make a pot of strong tea and add it to a bowl of water, at a temperature you find comfortable. Do this weekly. Rubbing the feet with surgical spirit can also toughen them up – don't do it too often, though, perhaps once a week, otherwise the skin can get too hard and crack.

Black toenails can occur as a result of shoes that are too tight, as the toes are pressed right up against the roof of the shoe. The blackness indicates that the nail has actually died and will come off. There will be a new nail growing to replace it, but you should also think of replacing your shoes. If this is not possible, you can cut slits in the shoes at the point where the toe was rubbing, but this is really only a temporary measure.

To soothe swollen feet, add three drops of lavender oil to a bowl of iced water.

If you are interested in using aromatherapy, there is a book by Valerie Ann Worwood which I have found indispensable: *The Fragrant Pharmacy: A complete guide to aromatherapy and essential oils* (Macmillan, 1990).

ACHILLES TENDON

The Achilles tendon attaches the calf muscle to the heel and is a common area of injury in distance runners. If you are not warmed up, or attempt a sudden burst of activity, the tendon becomes inflamed and sore to the touch. This condition is known as 'tendonitis'. Rest is really the only way to let the inflammation subside and the pain cease. Afterwards you will have to build up slowly to your former level of training. It is also advisable to run on a softer surface such as grass, when you get going again.

There is another form of tendonitis when the pain occurs at the point where the tendon joins the heel. There may be no swelling, but a continuous pain that does not clear up with rest. This can be caused by a sudden change in training, such as hill running, doing high mileage in shoes badly worn at the heel or generally overtraining. Women runners can suffer from this form of tendonitis if they usually wear high-heeled shoes. The tendon is required to do very little work in these types of shoes and is then suddenly stretched back to normal in running shoes. Some very experienced runners have found that this form of tendonitis doesn't clear up with rest and that surgery may be needed. Find out why you have developed this type of tendonitis; if it is for any of the reasons above, make the necessary adjustments and modify your training till the pain has gone and the condition has cleared up. Try swimming or cycling to maintain your fitness during this time.

ANKLES

You may suffer injury to your ankle from bad footing on uneven ground or from tripping on a kerb. The result is a sprained ankle, which is when the ligaments around the ankle are torn or ruptured. The severity of the sprain can vary and it is worth getting the ankle X-rayed to make sure that you haven't fractured the bone.

There is a simple procedure which can be applied to all sprains, denoted by the letters RICE:

R – Rest
I – Ice
C – Compression
E – Elevation

This means stop running and as soon as you can, apply ice to the sprained area (ice-cubes in a plastic bag or a bag of frozen peas will do). The ice will contract the blood vessels, prevent bleeding in the muscles and lessen inflammation. Apply the ice, six to eight times over a 48-hour period. In order to support the weakened ankle, use an elasticated tube bandage, folded double from the toes to the knee. Keep it on during the day, but not at night. Finally, raise the leg and support it in a comfortable position.

Arnica and Ruta creams have a very beneficial effect on sprains and are completely natural products. If the pain is very uncomfortable, use a painkiller that is anti-inflammatory, which you can get from a pharmacy.

Follow the RICE procedure immediately, as it really is most effective in the treatment of sprains. You will then have to judge the time you need to recover. Be guided by the pain and the ability of the ankle to support your weight. You may need to rest for anything up to 14 days, depending on the severity of the sprain.

Swimming is a good alternative to running if you have a sprained ankle. It is a way of maintaining your fitness without placing any stress on the joint. You can also mobilize the ankle by slowly turning it in circles, first one way then the other. When you feel it's time to start running again, invest in an ankle sport support, and use it when you're warming up, running and cooling down. Run on an even surface and avoid hills for a while until the ankle regains its strength. Most importantly, build up slowly – too much too soon could cause further damage.

SHIN SPLINTS

This form of injury is a sharp pain and tightness on the outside of the shin. It is caused because the shin muscles expand during running in a very restricted area and pressure builds up, leading to poor circulation. There are also a variety of other circumstances that may cause shin splints, such as:

- **high mileage on roads or other hard surfaces**
- **inflexible shoes**
- **poor cushioning in shoes**
- **running on the balls of your feet, instead of heel through toe**
- **leaning forward when you run as opposed to keeping the body upright**

All of these problems can be solved. If the pain is very uncomfortable when running, stop and put ice on the shins as soon as possible. Gently massaging the shins can also ease the pain. Once the pain has subsided and you have rested, it is best to train on a level grass surface. Make sure that your shoes aren't worn down, as this will increase the pressure on your shins.

CRAMP AND STITCH

Cramp is a sudden painful spasm of the muscles and feels as though the muscles are actually locked. The reason for it isn't fully understood, but it could be down to the loss of electrolytes (mineral salts) through sweating. It could also be due to the continuous use of the same muscle groups that occurs in distance running. The best way to deal with it is to stretch out the particular muscles and gently massage them till the cramp ceases. You will have to stop to do this. Changing your stride momentarily will also help.

I am particularly prone to leg cramp at night and it seems to have increased with running. To begin with I would leap out of bed and hobble around the room, stubbing my toe into the bargain and causing quite a commotion. Now if I'm woken with cramp, I just stretch out the leg gently and wait for it to pass, as it always does. Panic, I have learned, makes everything worse.

Stitch strikes in a similar way to cramp – suddenly – and is a sharp, tight pain, usually in the side, but sometimes in the shoulder area. It occurs for a variety of reasons: eating too soon before a run, taking on too much fluid before a run, needing to go to the loo or being anxious in a race. Whatever brings it on, you know when you've got it.

Don't stop with a stitch, keep running, even if you temporarily slow down. I find it beneficial to press firmly where the stitch is and to stretch out from the waist, so that I'm not slouching. If the pain is on my right side, I have found stretching my right arm up above my head seems to help the stitch to pass. This works on both sides.

KNEES

Knee pain is very common in runners and can be caused by a variety of circumstances. Check the alignment of the feet and make sure that they always land parallel, as problems will arise with splayed feet, pigeon toes or poor alignment in the legs with knock knees or bow legs. The runner may also over-pronate. This means putting too much weight on the inside of the foot as the foot strikes the ground.

Problems can also develop if the hamstring muscles are not fully warmed up or stretched before running. The leg isn't fully extended when running distances, shortening the hamstrings, so it's a good idea to change your stride and pace regularly, and include hill running, which gives most of the muscle groups a thorough work-out.

If you feel your knees are weak, build up the flexibility in the knee joint and strengthen the muscles above the knee – the quads – by doing the following exercise:

Sit on a table, tighten the bottom and stomach, and straighten out one leg at a time from the knee, flexing the toes up towards you.
Repeat this 3 x 10 times in each leg daily.

One particular condition – *chondromalacia patella* – is very common and is the wearing down of the cartilage under the patella (knee-cap) by the end of the femur (thigh bone). This kind of injury is due to repetitive overuse and may be brought on by any of the reasons listed above. When you think of it, the knee joint absorbs most of the shock of the body when running, and this is why good shoes and good alignment of the body will help to prevent injury in this area.

Always get advice with knee pain. You can apply the RICE procedure, which will give relief, and always use a knee sport support, once you start to run again. As with other injuries, build up gradually to your former level.

HIPS

Pain and injury in this area is caused usually by poor alignment in the legs in the same way as for the knees, by worn down or badly fitting shoes, or a habit of unevenly distributing the weight on the top half of the body. Problems could also be caused by running with one foot in the camber of the road, effectively making one leg longer than the other, thus throwing out the balance of the pelvis.

If the pain persists once you have eliminated any of the obvious causes, you may need to consult a doctor, who might recommend seeing a physiotherapist or osteopath.

You can prevent injury in this area by paying attention to the warm up and cool down exercises aimed specifically at strengthening and building up the mobilization of the hips. I particularly benefit from a yoga position – the triangle – and I feel I have run more smoothly and efficiently since I incorporated it into my warm up or cool down *(see pp.43–59)*.

Many experienced runners feel that although the legs do the work, the strength and balance comes from the hips, pelvis and lower back – i.e. the centre of their bodies – and the stronger they are in the centre, the better runners they will be.

THE BACK

Back pain may well occur when running, especially in the new runner and in anyone who is overweight. The reason is usually down to the fact that the muscles that support the back have become weak. It is quite natural to suffer some aches and pains as shock is absorbed in to the small of the back, but if the pain is severe, stop running for a couple of days, or until the pain has gone, soak in hot baths and use a heat rub. When you return to running, choose a soft even surface like grass, which will be less hard on your back than roads and pavements.

Common causes of backache are weak abdominal muscles and lack of flexibility. Apart from the warm up and cool down exercises, add sets of sit-ups to strengthen the abdominal muscles on a light training day. Running decreases flexibility, as it tightens the calf and hamstring muscles, which is why stretching after a run is so important. Flexibility can also prevent and relieve back pain, and the yoga position 'the cat' is very effective for the lower back *(see p.55)*.

Where to Go for Treatment

The first port of call for most of us with an injury will be the doctor. He or she will diagnose your injury, possibly send you for an X-ray and advise you on how to recover. If he understands that you are a committed runner, he may recommend that you visit either a physiotherapist or an osteopath, who will work with your body to enable you to run as soon as possible. There are now quite a range of practitioners in complementary medicine who offer various therapies that runners might find useful and here is a summary of those available. Contact addresses are listed at the back of the book *(see p.148)*.

Acupuncture

This is an ancient Chinese form of medicine based on the idea that there are lines of energy running throughout the body called 'meridians'. Illness occurs when there are blockages along the meridians and these can be unblocked by inserting needles at specific points. The needles don't actually hurt; as the point is contacted, there is a small tingly shock that isn't unpleasant. The treatment can also be given with lasers, for those squeamish about needles. Acupuncture can be used for treating specific conditions, as an aid to recovery after injury and as a means of de-stressing and relaxing.

Aromatherapy

This is the use of specific essential plant oils to promote well-being and prevent disease. They can be used in a variety of ways such as massage, inhalation and baths. There are specific combinations of oils that will relieve aches and pains, bruising cramps and inflammation. They can also de-stress the body and aid relaxation. Although you can buy the oils over the counter, it is best to seek advice, to prevent any adverse reaction.

Homoeopathy

The basic principle of this therapy is that like cures like. Practitioners will determine what is wrong through a range of questions and then treat you with the minutest dilutions of vegetable or mineral substances that in larger doses would actually cause symptoms similar to the problem. Homoeopathy is a subtle form of treatment and has a lot of success. It can treat all the muscular aches, pains and strains incurred in running, as well as offer prevention against colds and 'flu. The treatments are given as pills, powders, liquids and creams.

Massage

This form of therapy has long been recognized for its benefits for runners, either as part of a maintenance programme or after a long run. It can restore life to tired, worked muscles and break down the build up of lactic acid, as well as de-stress the body. You can often find a masseur who specializes in sports massage and will know just what treatment a runner requires. Some masseurs will use aromatherapy oils.

Shiatsu

This is an ancient Japanese therapy similar to acupuncture in that is based on the idea of meridians. However, instead of using needles, the practitioner uses his or her fingers, thumbs, elbows, knees, hands and feet to apply pressure and massage the blocked areas to release the energy. Shiatsu can be a very dynamic treatment, leaving you feeling refreshed and invigorated.

The four following therapies are quite closely linked, are hands-on therapies and deal with the musculo-skeletal system using manipulation of the body to bring about relief.

Chiropractic

This form of therapy concentrates on the relationship between the nerve tissues and the spinal column. It has a latent long-term effect on preventing injury, but can also deal with existing problems.

Kinesiology

Liz uses kinesiology to maintain herself in peak condition. Treatment is based on the idea that certain muscle groups are related to specific parts of the body. The kinesiologist tests the muscles by touch and deep massage in order to discover areas of energy blockage and imbalance. Using the changed muscle response as a guide, specific problems can be located and treated very swiftly. Sometimes in as little as two or three sessions, the therapist can alleviate problems that have persisted for several years. The treatment is also backed up with dietary advice.

Osteopathy

Osteopathy has long been viewed as a very efficient way of maintaining the body and treating specific injury. It is a treatment based on traditional methods of manipulation using a person's limbs and spine as leverages to untwist the body, naturally realigning it. An osteopath will also use massage during the treatment. You can find specific sports osteopaths who will have a very thorough understanding of sports injury.

Physiotherapy

Most people will have heard of this form of therapy and it may be the first choice when injured through sport. You can receive this treatment through the National Health Service and many physiotherapists specialize in sports injuries. It is a hands-on treatment dealing with the musculo-skeletal system, offering back-up pre- and post-operatively. The therapist will use heat, ultrasound or laser treatment, massage and exercise to rehabilitate the injured area. Look for a chartered physiotherapist with the initials MCSP or SRP after his or her name.

SPORTS INJURY CLINICS

These are just what the name implies and you can find details of your nearest clinic either from your running club, a good sports shop or the local phone book. A good clinic will use the process of dynamic assessment to discover not only the nature of your injury but how and why it came about, how best to treat it and, most importantly, how to prevent it recurring. To do this they will use a range of machines, including computerized isokinetic testing equipment which stimulates real-life muscle conditions in order to detect very subtle problems, make the right diagnosis and choose the correct form of treatment. Dynamic assessment looks at the whole person, not just the injured area. They will offer you a range of treatments from skilled qualified physiotherapists, osteopaths, podiatrists and sports masseurs. They can advise on future body maintenance and preventive measures, as well as nutrition.

A podiatrist is a doctor who treats disorders in feet. Many élite runners use a podiatrist to examine a recurring injury – for example a problem in the knee or back that may be caused by poor alignment in one or other of the feet.

At a consultation the podiatrist will record the runner on a running machine from the rear view and from the side. A very accurate assessment can be made from studying the gait and footfall, etc., as well as examining the shoes.

The podiatrist will then have an orthotic made. This is a plastic custom-made insole that slips into both running and normal shoes. The runner wears the orthotics all the time, thus bringing about a correction to the feet – in a way helping nature out by balancing the feet. Many recurring injury problems can be sorted out with the use of orthotics.

Sports injury clinics realize that as a runner, of whatever level, you will want to get back to running as soon as is realistically possible, and will devise programmes to maintain your fitness and build up strength, specifically for the injured area. They will suggest running related activities and flexibility exercises, taking a proactive approach and giving you guidance as to whether or not you should run.

LIZ: 'Being told I would never run again is probably one of the most difficult things I have ever had to face. I felt totally alone. Somehow the belief I had in myself, the support from my husband and family, and the knowledge that there was someone out there who could help me, pulled me through.'

Surely the worst scenario for a professional athlete and in fact anyone who runs and has had to take time off from running because of injury will tell you of the frustration and irritability they experience. One of the hardest things to accept in this situation is that you just don't know how long you will have to be out of action, as everybody responds differently to treatment. The best advice I have been given is to accept the situation for what it is, and to give in, as that will stress the body less and aid the healing process. To help me through these times I have taken up swimming so as to maintain a level of fitness and used relaxation techniques such as tapes and meditation to de-stress the body, with some success. If you have to take time off running, be creative and explore ways of maintaining your fitness, and helping the healing process. It really helps to have support from the people around you as well, because you do feel out of sorts if you can't get out to run and that needs to be understood. You're not an obsessive monster, just someone who likes to run and can't at the moment. So be of good cheer and rest assured that you will be out there running sooner than you think.

It's All in the Mind

It is a fact that a realistic yet positive mental attitude to running, coupled with a good training effort, will bring about success. As you work on your body to increase its fitness, so you can work on the mind to develop a constructive approach to running. Obviously some people are more temperamentally suited to endurance training than others, but with thought, and by being your own coach, you can be your own source of encouragement.

Having confidence in yourself is a huge asset in marathon training and racing. You can gain this confidence by choosing and adhering to a schedule that suits you, setting attainable goals and recording your progress. This way you are creatively in control of your training. Confidence can be undermined by sudden shocks and surprises, but if you have good foundations you will be less thrown by the unexpected.

Keeping yourself motivated over a lengthy period of time during training can be difficult. There are many external factors that will help along the way such as praise, completing races and collecting medals. However the most powerful force of motivation is internal – you are running for your own pleasure and personal achievement. This form of inner motivation will see you through the bleakest runs and most frustrating lay-offs due to illness or injury.

OVERCOMING ANXIETY

Stress and anxiety can be brought on by feeling overwhelmed and daunted by what you are actually attempting to do, especially in the cold dark days of winter training. Don't fear the worst; recap on what you have achieved so far. Each session will bring you closer to your goal.

Fear can actually be a very positive and useful motivator as long as it doesn't get out of proportion. Going into the unknown naturally arouses fear and anxiety, but these can be eased away by good preparation and training.

There is really very little difference between training and racing if you approach both in the same way – setting out to do your best. This workmanlike attitude can ease the anxiety. I sometimes say to myself before a run that it's OK if I have to stop. Consequently I never have, but I know I have the choice. Put it in perspective – I have it on very good authority that the world as we know it will not cease to be if you stop running!

NOW RELAX!

Finally, relaxation is the balance needed to counter mental and physical tiredness. Keeping to your schedule and achieving all your short-term goals will help you to relax and rest properly with less worry. If you are in control of your training and race preparation you will have a more carefree attitude and a relaxed mind, which will help you when you run.

You may wish to use relaxation techniques in order to switch off. Massage is wonderful for both mind and body. You can also use visualization techniques – calling up pleasant memories that evoke a calm, happy state. Colours and words can have the same effect. Self-induced or autogenic relaxation such as this has a direct effect on the body, relieving muscular tension.

Another effective mental technique to help you through the unknown, such as your first race or long run, is to 'dream' yourself through it. Break the distance down into runs you have experienced, so that the unknown becomes familiar. This is particularly helpful in the later stages of the marathon – beyond 18 miles, which I relate to a familiar five- and three-mile run, which I know I can do easily.

SUMMING UP

- Aim to prevent injury by having the best footwear possible and wearing the right clothing, especially in the cold weather as muscles need to be kept warm to perform well.
- Always warm up and cool down.
- If you feel particularly tired, whether from overtraining, work, or post cold or 'flu, do not train hard.
- Take care of your diet, drink enough fluids and get plenty of sleep.
- If you incur an injury, seek the appropriate treatment as soon as possible and familiarize yourself with RICE.
- Work out how long you think you won't be able to run and devise a programme to maintain strength, fitness and flexibility.
- When you return to running after illness or injury, be cautious and work up gradually to your former level.
- Relax and take it in your stride!

ten **halfway through**

you will notice that there is an emphasis to do a long steady run once a week – in this schedule on a Sunday, but if you need to fit it in on another day to suit your lifestyle, that's fine. To maintain your interest it is important that you vary your routes and you try to include as many different surfaces as possible when you run.

One good way of increasing the distance of your runs is to establish a route from home that is about five miles, then 'add on' a variety of other distances, such as three, four and six miles. This way you can build up different combinations of runs to ring the changes. Some runners prefer to work out a figure of eight type of circuit that always takes in their home, so that they can get a drink, peel off a layer of clothing, go to the loo or, well, if necessary, stop. This can be a very practical solution and you can build up the actual distance in the 'add on' way suggested above.

Now that you are building up the miles it is very important to drink regularly, which means carrying a drink with you or knowing where there is a strategically placed water fountain *en route*! Always carry a bit of cash on you, enough for a phone call, just in case you do get into difficulties and need to call home.

Running on a Variety of Surfaces

HILLS

Try to incorporate hills into your routes, as they are very beneficial to your training programme. Hill running is a very thorough work-out for the whole body and uses muscles in a slightly different way than when running on a flat surface by virtue of the fact that you are using your strength to propel you up an incline. The effect of this is to strengthen your legs, back and abdominal muscles.

If possible, when first introducing hills into your run, choose an easy hill and gradually build up to steeper hills. Attack the uphill slowly and pace yourself, keeping your breathing steady, then take it easy on the downhill. There is a tendency to let go on the downhill, but you do have to be careful of your footing as the momentum gathers, as there is a lot of stress on the shins and ankles.

You may be encouraged by your club to take part in strength training sessions on hills. This means running fast uphill and jogging slowly downhill, perhaps 10–12 times, in combination with an easy run. Do what you can. Remember improvement will come gradually, so don't do too much too soon.

Hills are important in building up mental stamina and there is a lot to be gained when you challenge yourself to tackle a hill when you are tired. They can be a much needed relief when you have been running on the flat for a long time – a hill affords you a change of pace and puts the body through a work-out which can be mentally refreshing just when you thought you couldn't go another step.

OFF-ROAD

Running off-road includes surfaces such as parks, woods, towpaths by rivers and canals, beaches, bridleways and public footpaths in the country. Your ability to run on any of these surfaces depends on what is available and hopefully your club will use routes that do sometimes take you off-road. You may eventually be running your marathon on the road, but running on softer surfaces has a less stressful effect on your body, so ring the changes as often as you can, even if it is only in your local park.

I can think of nothing better than to be able to set off for a run in Richmond Deer Park. It's glorious all year long, but my favourite time has to be autumn, running through all the fantastic colours as the leaves change and having a chance encounter with a majestic stag rising up out of the ferns. It is quite breathtaking and takes running into another dimension.

Being able to go off to a place of natural beauty can have a very therapeutic effect, particularly when you feel the going is getting tough and you are fed up with the miles of road running. The environment will have the desired effect, put wind in your sails and rekindle your flagging enthusiasm.

You may feel a little self-conscious going to the track, however it is a good way of testing your progress, as you can push yourself over a fixed distance and find out your mile speed. Most clubs will do track sessions, so it won't be hard to join in.

More experienced runners do interval training as way of improving. This involves running a lap at your fastest mile speed then jogging half a lap slowly to recover, then repeating the fast pace lap again. Repeating this up to 10 times will bring about great improvement.

Dealing with the Climate

We all respond differently to the weather, but you will notice as you work through your training programme that you will take a lot of interest in what the weather is doing. You will sometimes find yourself out running in conditions where previously you would have cancelled everything and stayed by the fire. On those days, probably the only other people you will see will be other runners!

The best conditions for running are cloudy and overcast, with a slight wind, preferably behind you, and you will discover that all the big international marathon road races are scheduled to coincide with these climactic conditions. Good weather on the day can make a huge difference to performance, as your body won't have to spend energy keeping cool or warming up, instead it all goes into your running.

Hot, sunny or humid conditions are the worst for runners and if precautions aren't taken, can be potentially dangerous. The body heats as you expend energy and it is hard to get rid of this heat on a hot day. You will sweat, but in humid conditions there will be less evaporation, so cooling by sweating is less efficient. You can help yourself in several ways. Wear light, loose clothing that will allow your skin to breathe, cover your head to prevent damage from direct sunlight, use a protective sports sun cream and, most important of all, make sure you are well hydrated. Take on plenty of liquid before a run, drink during the run and replace fluids afterwards. Drink when you are not thirsty; just keep topping up.

Running in the cold proves to be less of a problem, as the body will naturally heat up from the energy produced. You do have to make sure that you warm up thoroughly, though, and get the blood circulating and the muscles stretched before you set off. Cover up well while you do your warm up and once you get going you may find that you want to peel off a layer and tie it round your waist.

In these conditions, the windchill factor can make the temperature seem colder and running into a harsh headwind can be both difficult and demoralizing. If at all possible, start running into the wind, so that it will be behind you when you return. A rain-suit will also give you a protective outer layer against the wind.

There's not really a lot you can do if you are out running and the heavens open; of course it will be welcomed on a hot day. Rain-suits are effective, but sometimes you will get wet and just have to accept it. After a while you won't really notice it.

Running through snow can be exciting as long as you are sure of your footing, but during these conditions don't expect to do your fastest times. Black ice can be hazardous and catch you unaware, so stick to familiar routes, and if need be, run where the road and walkways have been gritted.

I find in cold, wet and windy weather it's a good idea to use a moisturizing cream on your face and on any other exposed skin, to keep you warm and prevent weathering.

SUMMING UP

- Plan routes with a variety of distances that you can 'add on' as the miles increase.
- Introduce as much variety as possible, combining off-road running, which is kinder to your bones and joints, with road running.
- Incorporate hills into your training programme, taking them slowly at first.
- Take advantage of track sessions suggested by your club. Alternatively, go off to the track yourself and do some interval training.
- If your spirits start to flag, take yourself off to a natural beauty spot and treat yourself to an easier, enjoyable run.
- Get out and run in all weathers. This will toughen you up and nothing will surprise you on race days.

eleven the last four weeks

in the first week of this training block you will be running your longest time/ distance so far of 150 minutes or 19–21 miles. Try to find a 20-mile race to enter (there are usually quite a few at this time) to make the run more sociable and enjoyable. Again, keep to your own pace and aim to finish steadily.

In total miles covered on a weekly basis you will not actually be running that much more than in the previous week, it is just that the distribution is different and you will be on your feet for the longest time to date. Follow the schedule closely. As you will notice, there is a tapering off of miles before the run. This will be repeated in the run up to the race and is a very important part of the training.

If you are not taking part in an organized event, decide in advance the route you are going to take for the run and make sure you are as accurate as you can be as to the distance, so that it doesn't exceed 21 miles. If possible, do the run at approximately the same time as the race, to accustom yourself to the similar demands of race day. This is an opportunity to try out the kit you will wear for the race and will give you time to make any adjustments. New clothes may chafe and rub, so it might be an idea to wash them through a couple of times to break them in.

You will need to be well hydrated before the run and it is worth spending at least a couple of hours beforehand topping up on water. Take water or an isotonic drink with you and work out where and how you can get drinks along the way. Stick to what you are used to and don't introduce anything that you haven't trained with before; I have known people to get quite sick trying out a different drink.

Fortunately in race conditions there's always plenty of running water.

When doing this run, it is handy to have a 'base', such as your home or the car or the clubhouse, to run from. When I do this long run, I follow a particular circuit that is 4.2 miles along the River Thames, incorporating two bridges, and I do five circuits, which is 21 miles. The car is my base, and I leave a supply of water and isotonic drinks there, plus a high-carbohydrate drink for afterwards as well as some bananas. I must admit the first time I did it I wondered if I would have any sensation left in my legs to be able to drive home! Somehow I made it.

Psychologically this run is very important as it will be the furthest distance you have encountered to date. You may not be running with a crowd so it is down to you to keep the motivation going. If you have put the miles in up until now, you will be in pretty good shape, however you may experience 'hitting the wall', which can make finishing very hard.

Hitting the Wall

The 'wall' occurs in the later stages of the marathon – usually between 18 and 23 miles. It often occurs on the Docklands stretch of the London Marathon. Without warning, running suddenly becomes incredibly difficult, your legs feel like lead, you have no muscle power and, worst of all, no mental push to help you through. You are in crisis.

The reason this has happened is that you have completely exhausted your main supply of energy – glycogen. So, in order to keep on running, the body turns to another source of energy – fat – to fuel your activity. The fitter you are and the more miles you get the body used to running, the more efficiently it will use both sources of energy. Endurance training has the effect of encouraging the body to use its glycogen stores sparingly, to burn fat and so to have a longer sustained source of glycogen, so you are running on a mixture of energy.

> **LIZ: 'I haven't really ever experienced hitting the wall and in fact I didn't feel good in the '95 London Marathon till about 23 miles. I haven't hit the wall because my preparation is so thorough and I've managed to keep my energy constant. I keep hydrated all through the race, drinking water and a light carbohydrate drink.'**

twelve countdown to the race

After your long run you will begin to ease up on the training and in the last week you will be tapering off quite dramatically. The reason for this is to allow the body to rest prior to the race and to recover from all the hard training you have put in up until now. It can feel quite strange to be running so little, so maintain your routine with short easy runs, just to tick over.

LIZ: 'I find the last week before a marathon the hardest part of the training, as I eat so much and am running so little. I get irritable and anxious at that time because I know I've got a hard race ahead of me. I feel the most unfit person in the world the day before the race!'

The Last Week

This period is crucial to your state of mind on the day. Ideally, you want to keep everything as ordinary and normal as possible. There will be one difference, though, which is that you will be running significantly fewer miles. You may feel the urge to go out for longer runs than scheduled, but resist the temptation – you are storing up all that keenness and energy for the race.

During this time of rest you can take the opportunity of building up the body's glycogen stores. Having followed the schedule, your body will be efficient in converting carbohydrate into glycogen. Here's how you can maximize that process in the last week.

TAPERING OFF AND CARBO-LOADING

Carbo-loading has been considered one way to increase your body's potential for storing glycogen. There is a scientific basis for this, derived from research carried out in Scandinavia. The idea is that after a hard long run, you refuel for three days on a low carbohydrate diet, followed by three days on high carbohydrate. The result is that you boost your glycogen stores beyond their normal levels. This may work for some runners, but it is an extreme way to treat the body. However, there is a modification to this process which works very well and is less stressful.

I prefer to follow a system which feels more normal and brings about a balance between tapering off and carbo-loading. While you are cutting down the mileage in the last week, you keep your diet the same for the first two days and then increase your carbohydrate intake over the following five days to about double what you would normally eat. This will gradually replenish your glycogen stores.

Tips for Eating in the Last Week

- **Avoid sugary carbohydrates such as cakes, biscuits, pastries and sweets, and emphasize complex carbohydrates such as cereals, wholemeal bread and pasta, potatoes and all vegetables, rice, beans and pulses. These foods will also naturally supply you with vitamins, minerals and electrolytes.**
- **If possible eat 'little and often', aiming to take on about 50 g of carbohydrate every two to three hours.**
- **Carbo-loading drinks are a good source of carbohydrate. They tend to be thick and syrupy, and are best sipped slowly two to three days before the race. Try them out during training, perhaps before the long run, and keep a note of how you felt in your diary. Don't introduce them for the first time in your preparation for the race.**

- Maintain your water intake of 2 litres/4 pints during the week, sipping all the time, even when you're not thirsty, so that it becomes a habit. That way you will be well hydrated before the race.
- Cut alcohol right out if possible, to help your hydration. You'll enjoy it all the more after the race. Also avoid any unusual and exotic foods that may have an upsetting effect on your system.

Suggested Carbo-loading Meals for One Day

BREAKFAST

125 g/4 oz muesli/cereal/porridge with semi-skimmed milk

2 slices of wholemeal toast

1 piece of fruit – preferably a banana

1 glass of fruit juice

SNACK

1 wholemeal salad sandwich

50 g/2 oz mixed nuts and raisins

1 apple

LUNCH

1 baked potato with baked beans

1 glass of fruit juice

SNACK

small pasta salad (about 225 g/8 oz), with kidney beans, sweetcorn and salad vegetables

125 g/4 oz fresh fruit salad

DINNER

125 g/4 oz chicken/fish/shellfish

125 g/4 oz rice/potatoes

mixed salad

1 orange

SNACK

2 slices of wholemeal bread/toast

1 tbsp honey

1 banana

Spend some time sorting out your kit-bag. You will need:

running numbers and eight pins
a towel
emergency money
a warm top
tissues
bin-bag for before the race
an energy drink
an energy bar and/or bananas
a sandwich
plasters
vaseline
liniment (if you use it)

REST AND RELAXATION

You have spent many months training your body to be able to run a marathon and yet running a marathon is definitely a question of mind over matter. Take time in this last week to reflect on your training – the highs and the lows. Look back through your training diary and remind yourself of the courage it has taken to get this far. You have dedicated yourself to an arduous training programme that requires discipline and courage to just keep going.

The last week can be very stressful, and you may notice that your moods are changeable and that your nearest and dearest pick up on this. It is all quite natural. To help you through, build in a quiet time for yourself every day to let your mind rest and relax. Listen to music or have a long soak in the bath – anything restful that doesn't require too much effort.

Some people choose to take time off work in this last week and I do think it's a good idea if you can arrange to be off work from the Thursday before a Sunday race. Take this time to be well prepared, to have all that you will require for the race sorted out and packed, and to ensure that you are happy with all your accommodation and travel arrangements.

I have experienced all the last week stresses and have also been aware of a quiet sense of excitement and exhilaration as I look forward to the race. One specific effect that the tapering off brings about in me is that I really want to run, I feel brimful of energy and have a terrific sense of well-being. Having trained so hard for so long, I can feel the benefit of the tapering off as my body becomes very rested and I can focus with pleasure on the race – after all, that's what it's all been leading to.

SUMMING UP

- Keep to the tapering off structure of the schedule and resist doing more miles.
- Ideally, do not run at all the day before a race. If you are a bit twitchy, go out for a very easy two-mile jog.
- Double your complex carbohydrate intake five days before the race and consume this in five to six small meals throughout the day.
- Increase your fluid intake to a minimum of 3 litres of water plus any other drinks. Avoid alcohol and unusual food and cut down tea and coffee.
- Arrange to lighten your workload and if possible take time off from the Thursday before a Sunday race.
- Keep your moods as even as you can, and spend some time every day alone and quiet.
- Get as much sleep as you can.
- Sort out your travel and accommodation arrangements in advance, and pack your kit-bag, including any particular food that you might need.

thirteen the big day

depending on the time of the race, make sure that you eat a small meal high in carbohydrate at least three hours beforehand. You may feel too nervous to eat, but you do need to top up your liver glycogen. Glycogen can only be stored in the liver for about 12 hours and is a necessary source of energy in the latter stages of the run.

Aim to keep your routine as normal as possible, and eat your usual breakfast, incorporating cereal and wholemeal toast with honey. If the race is in the afternoon, have a light breakfast and a light meal with low protein and low fat, again three hours before the race.

If you are staying away from home the night before the race, take a selection of the breakfast you would usually eat with you as it's best not to introduce anything different at this late stage. Don't be persuaded to alter your habits, no matter how well-meaning your host may be.

Anxiety has the effect of slowing down digestion, so try to relax after your meal and avoid rushing around. If you really can't eat before the race, take a meal replacement drink such as slimmers use or a carbohydrate drink two to three hours before the race so as not to start the race with a high blood sugar concentration.

Start to top up your fluids as soon as you get up, as you will have lost hydration while sleeping. Don't drink too much tea or coffee, as they have a diuretic effect.

Be prepared for a change in weather conditions. This can often be quite a surprise and you may need to alter your kit by adding or peeling off a layer.

Having worked out your route to the race, set out with plenty of time, aiming to get there at least an hour before the start. Although you may find there is a very exciting atmosphere, try not to let it deflect you from your preparation. You can find yourself stopping and having chats and suddenly 20 minutes have gone by and you're not ready.

If you are with a club, they may supply transport and a safe place to store your kit, otherwise the organizers of the event will offer secure storage. Strip down to your running kit, apply the plasters, vaseline and liniments, etc., store your kit then ... queue for the loo! This is a crucial activity and at some events can take up to half an hour!

Cover up before the race with an old sweat-top or black bin-bag so as to keep warm. You can discard it when you get going.

Keep a small bottle of water with you, sipping from time to time, until about 20 minutes before the start. You will be supplied with water on all races and some events will give you squash or a brand name replacement drink. Only use these if you are used to them in training, as they can upset your stomach. Some runners use energy bars and dried fruit to sustain their energy through the run; again, don't eat through the race if you're not used to it.

Allow yourself a good 10 minutes for your warm up and, despite your nerves, do it thoroughly and slowly. If you have to wait at the start, keep lightly jogging and stretching.

Set your own watch as you go over the start line, as it can be up to 10 minutes after the actual start gun, depending on the attendance at the race. That way you can monitor your own race.

Aim to run the first five miles at your predicted race speed. Being suddenly surrounded by a variety of runners can throw you off, so run your own race and don't worry about the rest.

You're off...

Enjoy the race!

fourteen ...and afterwards

so there you are with your medal, a space blanket, a goody bag, buckling legs and a daft grin on your face. What happens now? Funnily enough, that is one question you will not have to ask yourself, you'll just know what to do, whether it's to collapse in a heap and never take another step, rush to the loo, be sick or fly around like a mad thing rejoicing that you have made it.

Depending on what state you are in physically at the finish, do try to keep moving, even if it is only at a crawl, encouraging your system to move all the waste products out of your muscles so you'll be less stiff in the following week. Drink as much as you can as soon as you can, and if you can face food, eat whatever you brought with you. There will usually be refreshments available if you don't have anything. Having been through the effort of running 26.2 miles, your body will tell you what it wants, so just follow its lead.

A very long soak in a hot bath with a glass of whatever you fancy is probably the next best thing to do. Hopefully you won't have too long a wait before you can do just that. If, however, you do have a long journey ahead of you after the race, try to arrange to at least have a shower first to freshen up and relax your muscles. If you have to sit for a long time in either a car or train, keep changing your position and stretching your muscles, and if on a train, go for a walk. It is very easy to stiffen up quickly after the race, so keep moving.

> **LIZ:** 'It's great really – I always look forward to a marathon because it means I'm going to have a break after it. It's a good point in my year and I really enjoy myself and catch up with everything I've had to put on hold while I'm training.'

There are many schools of thought as to what to do in the week after the race. Liz has a complete and well-earned break, and indeed we all need to recover from the enormous strain of the build up and race. I find that gentle exercise and stretching are very beneficial during the first two or three days after the race to ease away the inevitable stiffness – after my first marathon I had to go up and down stairs on my bottom, I was so sore.

Only you will know when and if you want to get back out there running. For some of you this will be your one and only marathon, something never to be attempted again. Others may have come to enjoy running and won't now be able to imagine a life without it. If you do get going again, remember to take it very slowly to start with. Warm up and do a gentle jog for two to three miles, cooling down to finish.

You will have enough information now to be able to plan your own schedule, whether it is to continue to train and run the odd race, or just to run to maintain fitness. If you do decide to keep running, build up gradually to your former level of training and do not consider doing another marathon for at least three months.

Apart from recovering from the intense physical strain that the marathon has placed on your body, you also need to rest your mind as it will have been focused for so long on achieving your goal. You will have discovered by now how important a role your mental attitude plays in training and then racing and after the initial euphoria wears off there can be a sense of something missing because you are no longer focused on the structure of your programme. These feelings are quite natural and taking a break helps you to bask in your achievement and reflect on all your hard work. This time after a marathon can be very pleasurable because you don't have to get out there and put in the miles. Take a tip from Liz and enjoy yourself. Catch up with your social life, have a holiday, do nothing – whatever suits you.

fifteen personal stories

Liz McColgan – My First Marathon

My first marathon was also my easiest marathon because I was going into the unknown – my body had never been there before. I decided only five weeks before the 1991 New York Marathon that I was going to run it, so I didn't do any specific pre-marathon training at all. I think I did about three long runs, each of about 20 miles, then I simply went and ran the race. I had a tremendous result, winning in 2:27:32, which was then the world's fastest marathon debut. I thoroughly enjoyed myself – I experienced no fatigue whatsoever, I didn't hit the wall, everything just went really, really well for me on the day.

I decided to run the marathon because having won the 10k title in the summer at the World Championships, I was in great shape and everything was clicking. These peaks are rare in an athlete's career so I couldn't bear not to make the most of my fitness. Usually after a World Championship I would be resting and planning the next year's programme, but when I was invited to run the marathon in New York in November I didn't hesitate. It was an instinctive decision – everything was going so well, I thought what the hell, why stop now? A lot of people thought I was moving up too soon and that I would never finish, but I felt differently. Although I may not have put in much specific training for the event, I had always been a high mileage person – I run over 100 miles a week, even during the track season – so the distance didn't bother me in the least.

The 26-mile smile.

I couldn't believe how easy the race was. When you do a 10k the split times are much faster, so when I came to the marathon it was more like a jog. I found it hard to hold myself back – in fact I'm sure I could have run a couple of minutes faster that day! Once I had decided to go for the New York Marathon, I did do one key session to prove to myself that I could go the distance but otherwise I just stuck to my 10k training, maintaining what I had done all summer. The rest was sheer self-belief.

Since then I have tried different approaches, overrunning the distance to 30 miles and underrunning to 21 miles, but I now prefer to keep the longest run to about 22 miles, running at faster than race pace. That suits me best. I can run till the cows come home but that doesn't necessarily get me fitter or more prepared. Psychologically it may feel good to say to yourself, 'I'm OK, I've run 30 miles,' but wasted miles are wasted fitness. We all have our limits and knowing when to stop can be as important as starting in the first place!

What really made the difference in '91 was that I changed my training. Until the birth of my daughter Eilish in the November of 1990 my race preparation was very different. After the birth, I concentrated more on speed endurance training and it certainly paid off. Medically they say there is an improvement in a female athlete's performance after she has had a baby and I can't dispute that. But I'm not 100 per cent convinced that my improvement was only down to having Eilish. I firmly believe that it was partly because I had changed my training and partly because having a break away from athletics had changed my whole attitude – I was hungry for competition again.

Speed endurance suits me. It means that I run faster than race pace over a short distance: if your race pace over a marathon is six minutes per mile, then try and run 5:40 or 5:45 over a six-mile distance, take a recovery for a minute or two, then go again. It's all about running faster over shorter distances, so that when you go up to marathon distance and you go to your race pace, which may be 10–15 seconds slower, it feels comfortable. But you must keep the recovery periods very short!

To be a successful marathon runner, I think you need to be a successful 10k runner, and for me it has been a natural progression, but you have to suit the distance, both physically and mentally. They say women take to distance running because we carry more fat and can run at a slower pace for longer. I train with Peter, my husband, who is an international steeplechaser. When we run together I often struggle to keep up with him because he's faster and fitter than me and can run a sub four mile, so he slows down a bit, especially for the track training. What we usually find is that if we're doing a long marathon session I begin to catch up with him towards the end because I'm more suited to the distance. The further we go, the faster I seem to get!

When I run I always talk to myself, urging myself on, listening to my heart and my breathing, trying to relax, and in a race I listen to the other girls around me to see how they're feeling. I have developed an in-built clock, so that when I'm pushing to my maximum I can tell the distance that I've covered from my pulse. If I wanted to run, say, five miles sustained when I'm training abroad, then I could probably tell that distance from pulse and time alone. A lot comes from experience; I've been running since I was 11 years old.

Weekly Running Schedule from my Childhood

Monday	3–5 miles
Tuesday	200 m hills x 12
Wednesday	3–5 miles
Thursday	6 x 800 m on grass loop
Friday	3–5 miles
Saturday	Rest
Sunday	4,000 m time trial, cross country or race

I wouldn't say that I'm a natural runner because when I started running I was faced with a predicament: young girls were limited to running short distances so I had no choice but to sprint. I wasn't the greatest sprinter and didn't show much form – it wasn't until I got older, about 13, and could enter longer races, that I started to excel. I have always had to work very hard to maintain my form and that's why I wouldn't call myself a natural. I do have natural endurance, but I have always had to work to realize its full potential.

In terms of competition, there weren't a lot of races about for female distance runners until the 80s. I ran in the first women's 10k at the Seoul Olympics in 1988. It seemed that before then women were more interested in competing in what I call the 'glory' events such as sprinting or high jump. There simply were not enough entrants to make an endurance event really happen. And it didn't help that some people still regarded it as socially undesirable for women to be seen sweating and working hard. Now thankfully there are a lot more women competing in all areas of athletics and naturally some have turned to the longer distances. You would rarely see a woman jogging in the street 15–20 years ago, and if you held a women's 10k event 10 years ago you might only have had two or three women running it. 10k running has now become a very competitive event and people even seem to enjoy watching it!

In recent years I have experienced the frustration of injury. Such times are always difficult for an athlete. You are forced to take time out to recover, but you don't know for how long, and that makes you anxious, which in turn interferes with the healing process – it's a vicious circle.

I am now fully back to training and one of the things that has been introduced into my programme is a work-out with light weights. It takes about half an hour to do a circuit of low weights and high repeats – nine exercises in all – for upper body strength. I don't want to bulk up at all, but to keep the muscles toned I do the circuit three times without any break for recovery, alternating from arms to legs. That takes about 25 minutes, then I do three small circuits of sit-ups, star jumps and bounding, to strengthen the muscles in my ankles and my feet. I do these sessions only twice a week, on an easy day, because they are intense and I wouldn't be able to do them every day. When Peter first saw me do them, especially the sit-ups, star jumps and bounding, he was so astonished I think it wore him out just watching me! The bounding is great for the calves: you keep your ankles together and while simultaneously using your arms, jump continuously. It's great fun and really gets your heart rate going. Peter couldn't believe that I could go from one set to another with no recovery and although he can beat me when we're out training, he'll never touch the demon circuits! Grete Waitz, who is now my coach, introduced me to the body-strengthening exercises but I devised my specific routine myself. Eilish has already had a go at it!

I have massage every day and every second day I have a massage treatment for specific areas. This was devised by my kinesiologist in the States, Ger Hartmann, who then taught Peter how to do it. A kinesiologist looks at the muscle movement over bone and Ger can tell just by looking at me what is wrong – as an ex-runner himself he is very aware of the stress areas in a runner's body. Since my injury there are specific areas that need keeping an eye on and Peter now knows how to do that. I use ice after long runs because however fast or slow you perform, minute blood vessels can become torn and reducing inflammation will aid the body's repair processes.

Twelve weeks is my maximum preparation time for a marathon – any longer and I would run the risk of being too tired. That's what happened to me going into the '95 London Marathon. I did far too long a preparation, mainly because I had been injured and could neither do any speed work nor could I corner. I was restricted to the type of training I could do, so I chose to do very high miles. I went into that marathon overtrained and overtired – five weeks earlier I might have run a brilliant race!

About three or four weeks before a marathon I do a sort of dress rehearsal. I try out what I'm going to wear and I have specially prepared drinks placed at exactly the same points they will be on race day. Before the London in '95 my longest run was 23 miles. Funnily enough one of the hardest parts of training for me is the week before the actual race. I don't do any running but I have to keep eating and I end up feeling like the laziest person in the world! All that food and inactivity makes me irritable and the thought of what lies ahead makes me anxious, so one way and other I'm not the most sociable of animals! I go into hibernation, particularly during the last two days. I just sit around and relax and lie down and eat and drink...

The night before the race I visualize myself running it. Sports psychologists sometimes have to encourage athletes to do this but it's always come quite naturally to me. During the last five days, on top of my three daily meals, I eat high-carbohydrate, easily digestible snacks, then three days prior to the race I eat a lot more pasta and rice along with the snacks and with two days to go drop the snacks and have a carbo-load drink, which is the equivalent of 24 plates of pasta! As you may have gathered, it's possible to overeat, so always listen carefully to your own system. All through training, particularly during the last week, it is important to take on plenty of fluid to prevent dehydration. In that last week I drink at least 3 litres of water a day. Unlike overeating, I don't think you can drink too much. It's good to sip constantly until the body is used to taking on at least 2 litres of water a day.

Twenty-four hours before the race I need to be left completely alone. I seem to vegetate, shutting everything down and conserving all my energy, both physical and mental, for the adventure ahead. It's the way I am, drifting off into my own world, oblivious to everything around me.

On the big day I eat a light breakfast about three hours before the race – something that I would normally eat. I don't introduce anything new into my routine. I don't have any superstitions, but I always do the same warm up exercises and a light jog. That never changes, whether I'm running on the track or in a marathon. I will have already tried out the kit I will be wearing and I never wear new shoes – they will have been well broken in by now. I haven't really experienced hitting 'the wall' and in fact in the London in '95 it wasn't until 23 miles that I started to actually enjoy the race. I think I had overdone the carbo-loading and if anything I felt sluggish until then. 'The wall' is caused by total depletion and my preparation has always kept my energy more or less constant.

After the race I get ice on the sorest parts of my body, take on more fluid, eat and sip on another carbo-load drink, which very effectively replenishes lost energy and seems to make me less stiff the following morning. I soak in the bath and have a gentle massage to relax the muscles.

The next day I find that it's good to start moving again, so I'll do a light jog, say one to two miles, and then have a break to let my body completely recover. A marathon puts great stress on the body, so to ensure that I'm fully recovered I always take a complete rest. It's a high point in my year. Full recovery takes about six weeks and the first two weeks of training after a break are very important. I cannot get straight back to the heavy stuff. It's essential to build up slowly for the next race.

Obviously, unless I've run it before, each course will be new to me. I was unfamiliar with the New York course in '91, but the only part that I was really interested in was the last six to seven miles, because that's when I'm at my most tired and where the real work begins. These days I always walk this part of the course to see how it's laid out and to find out where the mile-markers are. All the courses are so different. Each one has its own distinctive character. To date I've enjoyed the New York the best, but that might have been because I was running like a demon at the time and when you run well everything around you looks and feels wonderful. The best thing about running the London is the support I get from the home crowd. The enthusiasm is infectious and in an atmosphere like that it's hard not to give of your best. When I'm running well nothing replaces the intensity of the track, but for sheer fun and excitement you can't beat road racing – I get a hell of a buzz out of it.

It goes without saying that there will be ups and downs in training, and sometimes you'll be left wondering at your inconsistencies. But if you just push through those downs the result of your efforts at the end of four weeks will set you up for the next four weeks. Believe me!

I'm a very competitive person, even at tiddlywinks! I have even been called stroppy, but I put that down to my upbringing. I was the youngest at home and hung out with my brothers. I wouldn't let them get away with anything. Whatever games we played I always struggled to win and that fighting spirit has stayed with me to this day. Mercifully, Peter is very laid back and easy going, which makes for a good partnership.

When I was a girl I felt no pressure from my mum or dad. I just went off to the athletics club one day and they were happy for me. They didn't come along to every meet and I don't think my dad saw me running till he came to the Dundee Schools Cross Country. I liked going to races on my own because I saw children who were made so nervous by the pressure from their parents that they became miserable and their performances suffered. Some would be crying and saying they only ran because they had to. Everything I've achieved I've done because I wanted to do it. I was lucky with my parents; if I came home with a medal they were delighted, but if not they were relaxed and welcoming. This was a very healthy attitude and allowed me to develop at my own speed. When I was young my athletic life was part of my whole social life. The club coach Harry Brewer had us playing what we thought were just entertaining games, but what he was really doing was building up the strength in our muscles while we were still young. He was really advanced in his thinking. He died when I was 19 but he had already instilled in me the ideas about training which I have built on since. He gave me a great foundation.

After the World Championships in '91 I took on too many opinions, began to doubt the very things that had been working for me and allowed new external influences to change my tried and tested working pattern. It's easy to take on too much information when you first start running and I think to run a marathon it's best to keep things simple and once you've decided what programme to follow, stick with it, then learn to listen to yourself and believe in yourself.

I think if I wasn't successful I would still enjoy running just as much. Sometimes I will go out with a problem on my mind and when I get back almost like magic it will have sorted itself out. Whatever level you're at, there's nothing better than getting out for a nice easy run – especially if the sun shines.

Running for me is a way of life. Six years ago I would have been paranoid about taking a day off. But I feel more balanced now. I have a more relaxed attitude and as I become older I have learned to trust the things that truly work for me, however strange they may seem!

My Pre-Marathon Training Schedule

	am	pm
Monday	7 miles	5 miles plus weights and circuits
Tuesday	5 miles	20 x 400 m jog 100 m recovery
Wednesday	5 miles	5 miles
Thursday	4 miles farther (varying distance and recovery 5 min–1 min)	5 miles
Friday	7 miles	5 miles
Saturday	18 mile run	rest
Sunday	10 miles	circuits and weights

On 21 April 1996 Liz proved all the cynics wrong when she blazed her way to victory, winning the Flora London Marathon. She had been told two and a half years before that she would never run again after a double knee injury almost ended her career, yet her determination and resilience have brought her resounding success. She has teamed up with her athletic heroine, the legendary Norwegian distance runner Grete Waitz, who has imposed quality for quantity, and is emerging as a less stressed and better technical runner.

I didn't feel particularly good at the halfway stage and I lost sight of the leaders, but as soon as I made the effort to get on terms I began to feel much better. By 17 miles I knew I was going to close the gap, but you can never take anything for granted. At this point a little girl ran out on the course and I might have tripped. You just never know.

Eamonn Martin – My First Marathon

The last thing on my mind going into the 1993 London Marathon was running. It had been completely overshadowed by the birth of our son just four days previously. He was actually due two weeks earlier, but as the race neared there was no sign of him. I told my wife that if he hadn't arrived by the end of the week, then I might not be able to be at the birth; I think he took that as a cue – and was born on the Thursday. I was in another world after that and somehow I had to pull myself round to concentrate on the race. I can't really explain it, but I had felt at least four years earlier that '93 would be my year for the marathon – I had actually set that in my sights in my training and my thinking. As I stood at the start line I knew this would be my race: I won in 2:10:50.

'I didn't feel a thing.' Victory for Eamonn Martin at London in 1993.

The crowd was absolutely fantastic, I've never known such support. There was never a moment when I couldn't hear people cheering me on. It was one of those days when you just float; everything was working and I didn't have to think about running – to tell the truth I don't remember what I thought about. Looking back I suppose the greatest thing about that run was how easy and relaxed I felt all the way through – no fatigue, no pain, nothing to hinder that glorious floating feeling. I don't know if that was because it was my first race at the distance and I was going into the unknown or because I had sensed during training that I was at a peak which gave me enormous confidence and a quiet feeling that 'today's the day – no one can touch me'.

As a 10k runner, moving up to the marathon distance was a natural choice for me and I still base my approach on 10k training, adding a long run once a week. I have always done high miles, my training being a combination of strength-endurance work and speed-endurance work; I've been running since my teens, so it's part of my life now.

I don't have a faddy diet – in fact I have strong feelings about the subject of sports nutrition and scientific methods of eating like carbo-loading. I think we eat too much in the West and I have witnessed magnificent sporting achievements by athletes from other countries who run on very simple diets. The magnificent Kenyans are a prime example of this. My own diet is quite ordinary. I eat and drink what I like, excluding red meat, and it supplies me with all the energy I need to run. I don't take on huge amounts of carbohydrate in the tapering off week because if I am dramatically cutting down my miles yet maintaining my diet then I am naturally replenishing the energy stores of glycogen. However the one thing I always do is eat 6 oz (175 g) of honey 36 hours before a race, to build up the liver glycogen. I read about this years ago and it does seem to have a positive effect.

One component of diet that can't be overlooked is taking on sufficient fluids. Here again I don't have any preference for a particular type of formula – I will happily drink whatever sports drink is provided during a race, but the best thing is water. In the morning before a run of 20 miles I will get up two hours earlier than normal to start the hydration process and I always plan my routes to incorporate water fountains! I couldn't tell you how much water I drink in a day, but I am continually sipping.

I do supplement my diet with vitamin C and zinc as a prevention against colds. I know there is no conclusive scientific research to back this up but I have recommended it to other runners in my club and they have all noticed less incidence of colds.

I like to keep everything about my running as natural and stress free as possible, so that I can easily adapt to the different circumstances that inevitably occur when you travel around the world competing. However we all have an Achilles heel and for me this was literally the case! Following two years of problems with my Achilles I was forced to have surgery in 1986. Touch wood, this was the only serious injury I have ever had to face, so I became something of a hypochondriac during my recovery period. Although I had rested thoroughly, training was very painful and in desperation I turned to more and more people for a cure. All this was to no avail until finally I had a consultation with a podiatrist. I had heard about orthotics before and having analysed me running on a treadmill he immediately set about custom-building me insoles for my running shoes as well as for my ordinary shoes. At last I had found the solution. Now I simply remove the neutral insoles from my running shoes and replace them with the customized orthotics. Not only was the pain behind me, but in 1988 in my 10k debut I broke the British record!

I have kept running diaries since I was at school and as I look back through them I can spot distinct trends. For example, one off day doesn't really matter, but if there are several bad days, these might signal the onset of a virus or an injury. I can also see periods when the training is going exceptionally well and I'm moving towards a peak. These simple patterns have proved invaluable to me when I am making training decisions. If I've simply got a cold, I can get out and run steadily, but if the cold starts to develop into something else, I have to make a careful judgement. Hard training at this moment could force the virus deep into the system and lead to a lot of time off. The four months I had out with the Achilles injury were particularly awkward in this respect. The situation was unprecedented for me so not only was I itching to get going again, but I had no personal experience on which to base my responses. At one stage I took up cycling, but it didn't feel right, so I resigned myself to the only real solution: total rest. I might have come to terms with this sooner if people hadn't constantly asked me how much I was missing running!

One thing that I really like to do about a week before a marathon is compete in a short, fast race; I really enjoy the sensation of going for it after the long marathon build up. That's what happened before the Chicago in October 1995. I found a 3k race in New York just a week before which I sailed through and then went on to win the Chicago in 2:11:18.

Eamonn's Running Diary

SUNDAY 24/9/95
Total miles: 25

Morning 10.00 am. Some stretching, drank plenty of liquid then 25-mile steady run on road. Weather mild but raining. I ran with company. I felt very strong, especially over the last five miles when fatigue sets in. Took a few drinks during run.

MONDAY 25/9/95
30 mins stretching
Total miles: 15

Morning 7.30 am. Five miles at a good steady pace on country – legs felt surprisingly good after yesterday's long run. Weather mild/dry.

Evening 7.00 pm. Meet at the athletic club. Three-mile run to church hill. Ten mins stretching then 20 x hill (130 metres) hard sprint up, slow jog down. I felt really fast and especially strong over the latter five – good sign after yesterday. Three miles warm down to finish. Weather mild.

TUESDAY 26/9/95
30 mins stretching
Total miles: 20

Morning 7.30 am. Ten miles at a really good pace over country. Weather mild. Ground conditions very good for running – a good spring in my stride.

Lunchtime. Visit osteopath.

Evening 4.30 pm. Ten miles at a steady pace over country/woodlands. I felt a little tired in the legs but only as expected after the last few days' training.

WEDNESDAY 27/9/95

30 mins stretching

Total miles: 15

Morning 7.30 am. Five miles steady run over country – I felt relaxed — legs were feeling good again. Weather was very mild – ideal for running.

Evening 7.00 pm. Meet at the athletic club. Three miles run to church hill, 10–15 mins stretch then 20 x hill (130 m) hard sprint up, slow jog down. I felt really fantastic – really fast/strong with an extra gear tonight. No one could get near me. Three miles warm down to finish. Weather mild/warm.

THURSDAY 28/9/95

30 mins stretching

Total miles: 20

Morning 7.30 am. Ten miles at a good pace on road and country – I felt good, flowing along, no real aches or pains from the week's training. Weather mild.

Evening 4.30 pm. Ten miles at a steady pace on road and country. I feel a bit lethargic due to high level of training intensity – muscles (quads) are a bit fatigued.

FRIDAY 29/9/95

30 mins stretching

Total miles: 10

Morning 7.30 am. Five miles steady run on road and country. Legs are a little fatigued but just ran easy to help recover. Weather mild.

Evening 4.45 pm. Five miles easy – steady run on road and country. I felt relaxed and ran well within myself. Weather still and mild.

SATURDAY 30/9/95

Total miles: 17

Morning 10.00 am. Meet lads at Thornden Park. Two and a half mile warm up followed by stretching for 15–20 mins then 5 x 100 m strides to get the legs turning over then session 8 x 3 minutes with two minutes recovery between. I felt really good, floating along and hitting really good markers at three minutes' effort. Weather was sunny and warm – ideal. Three miles warm down to finish.

Evening 5.30 pm. Five miles steady run on country. I felt good. Weather mild. Chance to reflect on a really good week's training as I start to back off slightly for the Chicago Marathon in two weeks' time.

Total miles this week = <u>122</u>

Cathy Shipton – My First Marathon

I was approached by the British Heart Foundation (BHF), an organization I had been involved with for about 10 years, in November 1994 and offered a place in the next London Marathon. Coincidence has always played a large part in my life and just two days prior to receiving this letter, I had been wondering how I could get a place in the London Marathon at this late stage. The BHF had been nominated as one of the official charities for the '94 London, so there was my running ticket – as if it had my name on it.

I had been secretly nursing a desire to run a marathon for about 14 years. As a student I lived very close to the start at Blackheath in south London. I remember a Sunday morning in the March of 1981 being late for rehearsals and not being able to get a bus. Why? Because they had all been re-routed to accommodate the first London Marathon! I was furious. I was late and nobody wanted to help – everyone was too busy joining the party and having a good time cheering on the runners. I did eventually get to rehearsal only to discover that everyone was as late as me and for the same reason. I would have probably got there quicker had I run!

Later that evening I watched news coverage of the marathon and was completely overawed by the whole idea of running 26.2 miles. Yes, there were some extremely fit looking athletes, but I was interested in the 'also rans' – people running for personal satisfaction, to raise money for charity or just for the hell of it. I made up my mind: one day I would run the London Marathon. You could have knocked me down with a feather (or a smelly old training shoe) when I opened the letter from the BHF and I didn't have to think too long about my answer – it was pretty much a forgone conclusion.

However, I would need help to train for and run a marathon, and the only person I knew who had ever run one was Chris, my partner, and his reaction to it when he finished was 'Ugh! Never again!' I asked him if he would just train with me and be my coach, but he said if he was going to do the training he might as well go the whole way and run it too.

At that time I was a very inexperienced runner – I called myself a 'plodder'. In the early days of my acting career I trained as an aerobics teacher – partly to keep fit and more importantly to keep solvent – but the only successful running I did was in a class or on a machine in a gym. My early attempts on the road usually ended after about a week. It was when Chris took me running in Richmond Park in the summertime that my outlook began to change. No roads or pavements, no people or cars to dodge, just beautiful open spaces with the odd deer to negotiate.

Chris ran regularly and well, and encouraged me to join in, doing whatever I could. He was always very supportive and knew just when to push me a bit further – usually when I was about to give up! Over a period of about two months I was regularly running a 4.2 mile circuit comfortably.

It had all fallen into place so easily – almost too easily. Some mornings I remember waking up and asking myself, 'What have I done?' Although deep down inside I had an absolute belief that I would not only start the race but finish it too, heaven only knows where that confidence came from. I couldn't think about the marathon without a thrill rushing through me, I was so excited. I was driving everybody mad talking about it. Fortunately for them, though, the thought of training soon brought me back down to earth. I decided to start serious training after Christmas and up until then I got out about five times a week, always running on grass, varying my times and not too bothered about distance.

I remember a gang of lads playing football on the sports field I used to circuit. Each time I passed them they would take it in turns to regale me with a feeble sexist joke. Although at first I rocked inside a little I refused to show it and after nine circuits even they had to acknowledge that there was not a wit among them. As the twilight fuzzed the edges of their football, their laughter dimmed and they eventually straggled homewards, leaving me to complete my run in peace. Average stuff for a girl runner and you learn to deal with it. This was just one of many tricky moments during my early training – a time when my late father was often in my thoughts.

Dad had died from coronary heart disease in 1985 at the age of only 63. That's why I became involved with the BHF. He had been incredibly fit and active in his youth – playing in the reserve team for Tottenham Hotspur, swinging a mean cricket bat in the summer and apparently showing great promise as a distance runner in his teens. As our family grew he seemed to have less and less time for sport, but he remained fiercely competitive and channelled all his excess energy into work. By the time he was into his 40s he was doing very long hours keeping a transport company together, smoking 60 high tar cigarettes a day, travelling everywhere by car and his sporting activity had been reduced to breeding and racing greyhounds! Dad had his first mild heart attack at the age of 57 and was encouraged by the doctor to change his lifestyle. Although he tried, and we all tried with him, the old ways crept back and as his health hadn't improved he decided to take early retirement. Sadly, he died 10 months later. We learned that several generations of men on Dad's side of the family had died young so there was obviously an hereditary weakness, but Dad had lived the longest and he would still be here today had he stopped smoking and taken even moderate regular exercise. I now believe we owe it not only to ourselves but also to those we love to learn about what makes us fit and healthy – I became involved with the BHF to draw people's attention to how they can literally save their own lives.

I found the first six weeks of my training particularly difficult. Chris ran set distances and as a beginner I decided to follow the advice in the marathon information pack and run set times, so we worked out routes that we could both follow. As I was slower than him, he would often push on ahead then loop back and rejoin me. He gave me simple advice and was very encouraging. One comment helped me in particular – he said that I seemed to have an easy running style but that I jutted my chin forward, as if I was trying to get there ahead of myself. He suggested that without becoming too conscious of it I should relax my head, neck and shoulders. This one observation made all the difference – I felt the tension release from my upper body, which of course indirectly gave me more energy and made running more enjoyable.

Obviously the aim of any training programme is to increase the workload and in the early days I often struggled. I can't deny that Chris sometimes got the brunt of my bad temper. You expect to have a few cross words teaching your nearest and dearest to drive, but try running the towpath with them in mid-February – I look back and wonder how he put up with me!

On some days the only thing that got me through was looking forward to crossing off another day's training in my diary. But I always felt good afterwards, and seemed to recover very quickly and have more energy than before. It didn't help that the early part of training was spent during the grey, dull cold days of a seemingly endless English winter. Oh, the joy when the sun broke through! We would often run with the dogs and their daft antics kept our spirits light, except when they took it upon themselves to herd the Richmond deer – that day the easy run turned into a fartlek!

Chris had said to me in the early days that he thought I would take to distance running but I remained unconvinced until about six weeks into training. Then came a big turnaround for me. I simply woke up one day and knew I was going to do a good run, even though – or perhaps because – I was attempting my longest to date: 11 miles. I had complete faith that I would get round. I went off on my own and felt like a runner for the first time; I really enjoyed the whole experience. I also made the changeover from running to time to running distance. Chris couldn't believe it, particularly when I returned home strong and full of spirits. I had timed it right both mentally and physically – a week earlier would have been too soon, but it also had to fit in with a planned half-marathon. I felt I was working with the training programme but not fighting my own instincts. Getting results that way is the best motivation in the world!

Something that I did quite naturally was to talk to myself all through the run and I wonder if this was an actor's reflex. When you play a part, you subliminally monitor everything you do outwardly and develop an inner dialogue. This happens when I run, to the extent that I am no longer conscious of it. I wasn't always conscious of the next six weeks either. It was a hectic time with intensive rehearsals for a play in Basingstoke, lightning dashes up and down the M3 and frequent dawntraining sessions. But somehow, and sometimes in spite of myself, everything flowed and tumbled into place. It's true what they say: 'The more you do, the more you can do.'

By this time Chris's father Phil had joined us to run the marathon – at the age of 67 – and had entered us in the Roding Valley Half at the end of February. We all did very well. I did 1 hour 59 mins, Chris did 1 hour 34 mins and his Dad did 1 hour 58 mins. I finished strongly, but not before my first experience of the dreaded 'wall'. It happened just after the eleventh mile (co-incidentally the longest distance I had previously run). Not only did I lose energy but, worse than that, I lost my will to go on. I didn't know what was wrong with me. This might sound extreme, but I felt suicidal. Then, remembering I had a bit of chocolate in my pocket, I ate it and within 100 yards the crisis had passed completely. In fact I went on to run the last miles quite a bit faster than all the rest.

From then on I started to experiment with different foods on training runs – things like glucose sweets, raisins, chocolate and apricots. I found chocolate too gooey and didn't like to eat it on the run and I felt happiest with soft dried apricots cut in half. I also always ate honey about an hour before a long run. But one area I don't think I paid sufficient attention to was hydration, and I now realize how much fluid you need in your system. I would take fluid on any runs over five miles, but I should also have been topping up during the rest of the day.

Chris, his dad and I set out on Easter Sunday to do our big 20-mile run. I think it took me about 3 hours 20 mins. On the last circuit I was cheered on by a family out for a stroll by the river and when I told them that I was on my twentieth mile they cheered all the more and two of the children even gave me a roller-skate escort!

In the week running up to the race I cut back on the training and bumped up the carbohydrates. This wasn't difficult as we tend to eat that kind of diet anyway, having fish or chicken only twice or three times a week. It would have been nice to have rested the day before but I had to do two shows – matinee and evening. The rest of the cast and crew thought I was hilarious, furiously stuffing food into my face every time I could make it back to the dressing room!

I still tingle with goosebumps when I think about race day: thousands of people from every walk of life descending on a hill in south London early on a Sunday morning with nothing much in common but the desire to run 26.2 miles! They have not come to buy or sell, they don't want to fight or talk politics, most of them aren't even interested in who wins. Male and female human beings of every shape and size from 18 to 88, selflessly, peacefully thronging together in a brilliant celebration of positive energy. Nerves crackle, minds leap, limbs pace and stretch, tongues wag unwittingly as every individual summons up his or her individual courage. Everyone is completely alone and all of us are totally together. The desire of the runners is matched only by the will of the crowd. The goodwill is almost over-whelming. I wish you could bottle it at its glorious source and take great gulps of it all year round. Given this highly charged atmosphere, it's a good idea to leave your-self plenty of time to pack your kit away and queue for the loo! The minutes just fly by, especially if you're a softy like me and you've got a lump in your throat.

Because of the crowds I took seven minutes to get across the start line and 12 minutes to do my first mile. Chris and I stayed together for two miles, then he pushed on to run at his own natural pace. It was at about this point that I palled up with a chap called Phil who, like me, was running for the first time. Our stride pattern seemed to be compatible and we went along together. Looking back I think of Phil as a guardian angel – he was always just there and seemed to know instinctively when I was finding it tough. We made the halfway point at about 2 hours 5 mins, a bit slower than I'd hoped, but considering the slow start and first mile, I was not disappointed.

The weather that day was very cold – apparently the coldest they had ever had for the race – and oh, did my spirits drop around the Docklands loop. I think everyone felt it. The crowds thinned out, the jazz bands faded, the wind gusted and the sky hung low. At one point I urged Phil to go on, but he just fell in with my pace until gradually we could build up again – he was a true gentleman.

The most emotional point during the race came at the Tower of London. The route takes in a historic cobbled walkway, which is perfect for an ambling tourist but grim for a blistered runner, and at 23 miles it feels like pure torture. As my poor tired joints struggled to cope with the cobbles, I looked up and saw a one-legged runner on crutches, overcoming these awful conditions. Suddenly my perspective changed, tears welled in my eyes and I knew that I would complete the run.

Unbeknown to me, my sister Christine and friends had positioned themselves by Big Ben, from where they managed to pick me out; the sound of their voices put wind in my sails. Phil and I really sprinted home – he even let me go through first. We finished in 4 hours 12 mins.

The organization at the end of the race is superb, and I quickly gathered my gear and met up with Chris, who had done 4 hours 8 mins. Then it was off to the pub for a Guinness and home by tube, glowing and swinging our medals.

The following day I travelled to Torquay to start a 12-week UK theatre tour. My poor mum hadn't believed that I would finish and when I rang to tell her, she was convinced I had dropped out. She's still not too sure about this running lark – she says, 'It jiggers your insides!' I took myself for a gentle jog the very next day and any stiffness soon passed. The feeling of achievement fortunately lasts a lot longer. In fact it was the euphoria of running in the '95 London that inspired me to write this book. Having risen to the challenge, I felt I could make anything happen!

Writing this book and working with Liz has brought about a slow transformation in my attitude towards running. I consider myself a fun runner, yet I decided in my training for the '96 Flora London Marathon that I should be able to do the thing I was writing about if I was to have any street-cred, so I upped the ante and put myself on the improvers' schedule ... with the outcome that I ran my best personal time of 3:45:15, in extremely hot weather conditions.

I followed the programme very closely and was delighted when slowly but surely all my times over distances came down because I was getting stronger and more efficient. I remember Liz saying that sometimes when you feel your pace slacken and you feel a bit tired, don't slow down, push faster. I found myself naturally doing this and was amazed at what I had in reserve. I started taking water or a sports drink on my longer runs and because my diet seemed to be sufficient, I found that I no longer needed any sustenance while I was running – all these improvements were a signal to me that my training and preparation were working for me.

Something that really kept me going was my diary. I would constantly compare my performance, noting down how I felt, what the weather conditions were like and any changes, good or bad, I noticed during the run. I found the more I did, the more I could do, to the extent that now the race has been run and I've had a rest, I'm back out there aiming at a 10k and half marathon every three to six weeks and enjoying keeping my weekly miles at about 30–35, so that next year ... who knows?!

I don't think I live to run, but I certainly run to live. My whole quality of life and health has improved since I started running. Because I run regularly, I eat what I like and after 20 years of dieting that's like being let out of jail! Sometimes if I'm faced with a difficult situation, I think of the courage and discipline it took for me to do the run and I look at things differently. The benefits are far-reaching and often unquantifiable: running is inexpensive and the time it takes is as nothing compared to the benefits it brings. But don't take my word for it. Feeling is believing and if you're anything like me, running is a feeling it's hard to do without.

sixteen the heartrunners' runs

i became involved in marathon running through the British Heart Foundation, as have many people. Here are their stories and tips, which I'm sure you'll find encouraging, heartwarming and informative.

Leslie H. Bolton
HERTFORDSHIRE

I am a 67 year old who has completed the London Marathon eight times, plus other marathons and runs, including the Tettenhall 'Tough Guy'.
So how does a 60+ tackle running 26.2 miles?
  I started running when I was in the army, cross-country and three-mile track. I laxed a bit after leaving the service, but took up running again in my early 50s when marathon running became popular.
  Considering I had the heart, lungs and legs of a 50 year old, I adopted a 'steady as she goes' approach, running alternate days, using the fartlek method of running a little, walking a little, then increasing the running and shortening the walking, and eventually increasing the distance.
  I found mental discipline very important and tried not to get carried away thinking I was as fit as the youngsters. I had to hold myself back and let them go. I found it very necessary to maintain a steady pace and that way I could also be a

source of encouragement to new runners, who were happy to stay at my pace. I could see them thinking, 'If he can do it, so can I.' What is most important for first timers is that they get around the course with as little discomfort as possible – personal bests will come later.

It is tempting to take time off work after the run, but go in, show off your medal and share the whole experience – people are very interested. It will also get you up and about and keep your limbs moving.

I get back to running gradually, but I don't stop, and capitalize on all that strength and endurance I have built up by planning for the next marathon.

Andy Mitchell
HULL

I completed my first London Marathon in 1995. Up until 1993 I had regularly played football and squash and was considered by many to be the fittest player at the squash club. But then, when I was only 38, I suffered chest pains whilst out running and to cut a long story short, I had heart by-pass surgery on 26 January 1994.

During my period of recuperation I was planning what sporting activities I would be able to participate in. Having discussed the matter with my GP, I decided that the marathon would be the ultimate test of endurance, the completion of which would signify my complete recovery. The marathon run would also give me the opportunity through sponsorship to raise money for the British Heart Foundation, without whom I would not be here today, and certainly not enjoying the quality of life I currently enjoy.

On my first day back at work on 12 April, I ran the three miles home – slowly – and I continued to do this two or three times a week till 1 May, which was the official start of my training.

I decided the only way I could focus my mind on the training was to set myself monthly targets and I aimed to build up the distance I could run over the coming months in this way: June: 5 miles, July: 9, August: 10, September: 10, October: 12, November: 14, December: 14, January: 16, February: 18 and finally March: 18. The effect was designed to build up gradually and not put too much stress on my leg muscles by gently increasing the mileage.

I would only complete the set distance for that month once a week and I didn't time myself; the important thing for me was to finish, the time was of no significance and would only be an added pressure.

During my first long runs I quickly realized that to follow the same route till March would be dull, so I worked out seven or eight different routes which I rotated. Going over routes I had used early on in training proved to be a way of assessing my progress which built up my confidence and enthusiasm as the race neared.

By completing monthly targets I did not put myself under pressure to complete every training session if I felt too tired or if the weather conditions were too hazardous. I could miss training rather than risk injury, knowing that I could make it up.

I didn't feel that one long training run a week was sufficient to enable me to run a marathon and in the early months I would cycle a variety of routes, building up the stamina in my legs, which had lost strength during my illness, without too much stress. I also continued my three-mile run home after work, but at a faster pace.

I occasionally did some sessions at a track, attempting to pace myself to eight-minute miles, which would be quicker than my anticipated race. At these sessions I never ran for more than five miles or 20 laps, at which time boredom set in. I would complete the session with sit-ups and press-ups to build up my upper body strength.

It was very important to build rest days into my programme and to ensure that no matter how tempting it was to run, I did actually rest. I always had a rest day after my long run. In the early days I alternated training days with rest days, but by Christmas I was training up to five days a week.

I always left a good gap after eating before I ran and made sure that I drank a lot of water, taking water with me in a bum-bag and making sure that I passed water fountains on my long runs. My diet was pretty normal, with slightly more carbohydrate, and I increased that considerably during the last week. On the day of the race I started drinking water as soon as I got up, knowing that there would also be water and Isostar offered all along the course – as well as loos.

At the start of the race there is a great excitement as new runners receive advice from those who have run the course before. For months you have been training the body to run 26.2 miles, but now the race starts in your mind and I decided to set myself targets along the route to keep me focused.

My first target was mile 1, but with hindsight it should have been to get to the start, because it took me eight minutes to reach the start line! It took me 10 minutes to run the first mile and I set my sights on the first water station at three miles. My next target was five miles; the first Isostar station. By that time my pace had picked up to nine-minute miles.

The next target was at six and a half miles, just by the Cutty Sark, which was a very impressive sight. Having now completed 25 per cent of the run and feeling fresh, I looked forward to nine miles which was a third of the way. My following target of 12 miles took me into double figures and the Tower of London. Just a short distance after that was the halfway stage; having completed the first half, I felt there was no reason why I shouldn't complete the second. It was also encouraging that now I would be counting down to my final target as opposed to counting up. My remaining targets were at 15, 16, 18, 20, 22 and 24 miles.

I had never run beyond 18 miles before, so to help me through this unknown territory I looked at the end of the run as an eight-mile training run that I had completed several times during my preparation. What also helped me is that the course goes past so many interesting landmarks and these take you out of yourself.

I finally completed the run in 4 hours 19 minutes. By splitting the race into smaller races and thinking no further than the completion of each section, I was able to finish feeling fairly comfortable. I drank from very early on in the race, even if I didn't want water. I also splashed water over myself to keep cool.

During the race I met and ran with a number of people, talking as we went. I had never met these people before and I remember there was one particular stage between 15 and 23 miles when their company really helped my mental attitude.

After the race I experienced feelings of pride and achievement such as I have never felt before. I had prepared fully for the race, but not for what came after with the long drive back to Yorkshire. I travelled with my children up the M1 and was feeling fine – until we stopped at a service station. It seemed most of the runners had converged at the northbound service station, so we decided to walk over to the southbound side. Climbing the stairs was absolute agony – my legs were like lead, probably because I had been sitting driving in one position. I think that is why, despite all the hot baths, it took so long for the stiffness to wear off the following week.

Gill Phillips
CAMBERLEY

The first year I ran the London Marathon was 1995. I did so in memory of my partner, who died of cancer the year before at the age of 47. Most of my sponsorship went to the Cause for Hope Appeal and some went to several other causes, including the British Heart Foundation.

I ran the marathon jointly with my boss, who supported most of the same charities as I did. We felt joint sponsorship would bring some interest from our work colleagues.

I am lucky enough to have a couple of friends who are runners – Malc, with whom I worked, and Rosemary, his wife, who is a former British athlete. They advised me and to begin with came with me to a club in Chinatown where I started weekly training, getting up to distances of three and four miles in only a few weeks. Although 50 years of age, I am reasonably fit and have been involved in sport since leaving school.

On hearing I had been accepted for the marathon, I started training 'in earnest' in December '94 – Boxing Day, actually. The training then stepped up to five days a week, running four or five miles daily and building up each week on the long runs to 8, 10, 14, 18 then 20 miles, always at a pace that suited me.

I am lucky to have a measured mile distance round a park where I work, which, although perhaps what could be termed 'boring' to some people, actually suited me. It meant if I felt the necessity I could stop, get a drink from inside the building or something to eat, use a toilet or go back to my car to sit without ever being too far from the necessary facilities.

My recovery usually meant sitting for half an hour in the car, to rest, eat or drink, and always going home to spend about an hour and a half in bed after a long run with the phone off the hook, often not sleeping but just resting.

My way of getting round the route was to say to myself, 'I won't start a mile unless I'm prepared to finish it!' This psychology worked for me and I think psychology has as much a part to play as fitness in completing the course.

Despite all this, however, I did experience great difficulties over the last six miles, which means that I will have to put even more effort in when I enter next year.

Philip Talbot
COVENTRY

The London Marathon 1995 was my first and the fulfilment of a dream for me. It was an experience that I would love to repeat, but my legs are beginning to feel their age and it wouldn't be fair to my wife, who got a lot less help around the house during the preceding six months!

The Tower of London.

I am now 44 and have had a life-long heart condition which, although hasn't caused me any real problems, has limited what I thought I was physically capable of achieving.

A few years ago, with a bit of encouragement from a work colleague, I started jogging. Having at that time never run more than about a quarter of a mile without stopping, I learned that by running at a slow pace and with a gradual build up I could run much further than I had thought possible.

I entered fun runs and then road races, and eventually I began to believe that with a determined training effort perhaps I could manage a marathon. I wanted my marathon to be a high profile one, which meant the London.

I used a street map to plan my routes and coloured each route differently, and I set myself a goal to run along as many roads as possible till the whole map was coloured in. I kept the street plan in my office at work and I could accurately work out the distances of each route. I was able to plan new routes and as the weekly mileage increased I made a conscious effort to run new streets so I could colour more of the plan. The aim of adding a new bit on every run maintained my interest and added variety, and acted as an incentive to get out and run.

When I ran the actual race I had my name printed onto my T-shirt. I had heard that this was a good thing to do as spectators would encourage you by name. How true I found this to be. It was just like having your own private army of supporters all around the course. I would look over to where I heard my name called and get a wave or a cheer. It seemed so warm and genuine I often asked myself, 'Do I know these people?'

The encouragement that this gave me was probably the most memorable aspect of the marathon for me. Mind you, it did have its downside in the second half, when I would occasionally walk and the crowd got on to me to start running again. When I did I was rewarded with more encouraging cheers.

I completed the run in 4 hours 44 minutes – plus seven minutes to cross the start line!

I was very sore after the race, and tended to avoid steps, stairs, hills and slopes as best I could. In the hotel we stayed at in London, it was easy to see who had just run the marathon, even if they were not wearing the T-shirt or medal!

I raised over £1,000 through sponsorship, but the most important thing was the sense of achievement and personal satisfaction that completing the marathon gave me.

further information

Running Magazines

Runners World – monthly
Today's Runner – monthly
Athletics Weekly – weekly

All the above have comprehensive race diaries throughout the year and information about running clubs, and can be obtained from good newsagents.

Calendar of World Marathon Events

Disney Marathon	January
Las Vegas Marathon & Half	February
Los Angeles Marathon	March
Two Oceans Ultra, Cape Town	April
Vienna Marathon	April
London Marathon	April
Paris Marathon	April
Rotterdam Marathon	April
Vancouver Marathon	May
Turin Marathon	May
Boulder Bolder, Colorado	May
Stockholm Marathon & Half	June
Comrades Marathon, Durban	June
Brugge Vets Wava Champs	June
Midnight Sun Marathon/Half/10 km	July
San Francisco Marathon	July
Swiss Alpine Events, Davos	July
Pikes Peak, Colorado	August
Medoc Marathon	September
Jungfrau Marathon	September
Amsterdam Marathon/Half/10 km	September
Paris–Versailles	September
Berlin Marathon	September
Paris 20 km	October
Reims	October
Lausanne Marathon/Half/10 km	October
Chicago Marathon	October
New York City Marathon	November
Florence Marathon	December
Barbados Marathon and 10 km	December
Honolulu Marathon	December

useful addresses

Acupuncture
The Council of Acupuncture
179 Gloucester Place
London NW1 6DX

Tel: 0171-724 5756

Aromatherapy
Aromatherapy Organisations Council
3 Latymer Close
Braybrooke
Market Harborough
Leicestershire
LE16 8LN

Tel: 01858 434242

Chiropractic
The British Chiropractic Association
Equity House
29 Whitely Street
Reading
Berkshire
RG2 0E9

Tel: 01734 757557

Homoeopathy
The Society of Homoeopaths
2 Artizan Road
Northampton
NN1 4HU

Tel: 01604 21400

Kinesiology
The Association for Systematic
  Kinesiology
39 Browns Road
Surbiton
Surrey
KT5 8ST

Massage
British Massage Therapy Council
Greenbank House
65a Adelphi Street
Preston
Lancashire
PR1 7BH

Tel: 01772 881063

Osteopathy
Osteopathic Information Service
PO Box 2074
Reading
Berkshire
RG1 4YR

Physiotherapy
The Chartered Society of
  Physiotherapists
14 Bedford Row
London WC1R 4ED

0171-306 6666

Shiatsu
The Shiatsu Society
5 Foxcote
Wokingham
Berkshire
RG11 3PG

Tel: 01734 730836

The British Heart Foundation
14 Fitzhardinge Street
London W1H 4DH

Tel: 0171-935 0185

further reading

Bean, Anita, *The Complete Guide to Sports Nutrition*, A & C Black, 1996

Carroll, Dr Stephen, *BUPA Family Guide to Healthy Living*, Dorling Kindersley, 1992

Gillie, Oliver, and Raby, Susana, *ABC Diet and Body Plan*, Hutchinson, 1984

Henderson, Joe, *Long Slow Distance: The humane way to train*, Anderson World
        Publishing, 1969

Isaacson, Cheryl, *Yoga Step by Step*, Thorsons, 1986

Martin, David, E., and Coe, Peter, N., *Training Distance Runners*, Leisure Press, USA,
        1991

Ridgeway, Judy, *Food for Sport*, Boxtree, 1994

Temple, Cliff, *Marathon, Cross Country and Road Running*, Stanley Paul, 1990

Tulloh, Bruce, *Running your First Marathon and ½ Marathon*, Thorsons, 1989

Wootton, Steve, *Nutrition for Sport*, Simon & Schuster, 1989

Worwood, Valerie Ann, *The Fragrant Pharmacy: A complete guide to aromatherapy
        and essential oils*, Macmillan, 1990

list of photographs

Text

Colour section

© Great North Run – Howard Boylan/Allsport
© The feelgood factor – Allsport
© 1993 New York Marathon – Darrell Ingham/Allsport USA
© 1996 Flora London Marathon – Tim Mathews/Allsport
© Raining medals – Ben Radford/Allsport
© Time weighs heavily – Colorsport
© 1996 Flora Wheelchair London Marathon – Stu Forster/Allsport
© 1995 BUPA Great North Run – Phil Cole/Allsport
© Afterglow – Ross Kinnaird/Allsport
© 1993 Nutrasweet London Marathon – Colorsport
© Sunshine Superman – Ben Radford/Allsport

index